David Thorns was born in County Durham in 1943. After graduating in Sociology from the University of Sheffield in 1964, he spent a year at Nottingham University as a Research Assistant in Rural Sociology, and is now Senior Lecturer in Sociology at the University of Auckland, New Zealand.

Suburbia is published in a sociology series under the general editorship of Professor John Rex.

David C. Thorns

Suburbia

Paladin

Granada Publishing Limited
Published in 1973 by Paladin
Frogmore, St Albans, Herts AL2 2NF

First published by MacGibbon & Kee Ltd 1972

Made and printed in Great Britain by
Richard Clay (The Chaucer Press) Ltd
Bungay, Suffolk
Set in Monotype Ehrhardt

Contents

Acknowledgements

We wish to acknowledge permission from the following publishers to quote from copyright works:

Jonathan Cape Ltd. and Simon & Schuster Inc. for permission to quote from *The Organisation Man* by William H. Whyte; Routledge & Kegan Paul and University of Toronto Press for permission to quote from *The Impact of Railways on Victorian Cities* by J. R. Kellett; Prentice-Hall Inc. for permission to quote from *Class in Suburbia* by William M. Dobriner; Basic Books Inc. for permission to quote from *Crestwood Heights: A Study of the Culture of Suburban Life* by John R. Seeley, R. Alexander Sim and Elizabeth W. Loosley; Columbia University Press for permission to quote from *The Suburban Myth* by Scott Donaldson; University of North Carolina Press for permission to quote from 'Fringe and Suburb Confusion of Concepts' by R. A. Kurtz and J. B. Eicher, which appeared in *Social Forces*, Vol. 37, 1958–9; Martin Secker & Warburg Ltd. and Harcourt Brace Jovanich Inc. for permission to quote from *The City in History* by Lewis Mumford; and The Society for the Study of Social Problems for permission to quote from 'Suburbia – New Homes for Old Values' by T. Kstanes and L. Reissman, which appeared in *Social Problems*, Vol. 7, 1959–60.

List of Illustrations

Preface

This book emerged out of a desire to bring together and to produce some order into the discussion about the role of the suburb as a new form of urban living and as an initiator of a new way of life. The arguments in this particular area have so often lacked evidence and sociological depth; these in some small way I have attempted to provide. However, in the end the book raises as many questions as it solves but does try to provide the basis upon which future research might be conducted in a more systematic and sociologically grounded way.

Acknowledgements are due to Aerofilms Limited and to the Keystone Press Agency for permission to reproduce their photographs.

I would also like to express my thanks to Professors G. D. Mitchell and J. Rex for their helpful criticisms and comments on an earlier draft of this book. Finally I would like to thank my wife without whose support and encouragement the writing of this book would probably never have taken place.

David C. Thorns, *University of Exeter*

1 Introduction

The most characteristic feature of present-day urbanism in most of the advanced industrial nations, unlike the past, is that of city dispersion, of the outward movement of the population from the city to the surrounding area. The people move out to the suburb, to the land of the semi-detached, the new housing estate, the new town, swamp the old rural villages and turn them into dormitories. The suburb, the description given to these mushrooming surrounds to our cities, has been a term which has never been free of controversy. Those who have written about it, lived in it, built or designed it have invariably had strong feelings either for or against it; they have seen it as the saviour of the population from the worst of city living or as the destroyer of the individuality of the population by its insistence upon conformity and the promotion of status divisions, competition and upward mobility striving. The surburbanite is seen as the leading example of the mass-produced man. The source of much of this controversy has to be sought not in the actual facts available about suburban life, but much more in the realm of the history of ideas.

The trend towards urban dispersal has led to the shift of the ideological controversy from the city–rural conflict to the city–suburban. In order to understand the latter adequately, the former must briefly be considered. The earliest attackers of city and urban life were those who saw the city as the source of all that was evil and corrupting in life as against the rural life which was the repository of all virtue. This position in American writing on urban life is typified by Thomas Jefferson, with his famous view of the city 'as pestilential to the morals, health and liberties of man'.[1] The virtues of rural life were also extolled by the Romantics who desired the 'wilderness', who were opposed to the organized life which was the inevitable consequence of urban development. The yearning for the simpler, rustic, pleasures to be found in the pre-urban days when the population lived in villages and were healthier and morally and spiritually more upright has had considerable influence upon thinking within Britain about the urban environment. This view is reflected in the writing of S. J. Low where he says:

For the bulk of humanity the life of rural labour is, no doubt, the happiest life . . . We recollect how even the leaders of Englishmen have come most often from the village rectory, the country house and the farm . . . Something there is, it is true, which 'the land' gives to those who live on it and by it, that cannot be produced under the more artificial conditions of life in the vicinity of a great town.[2]

The thread running through Low's discussion is that the city will inevitably lead to the weakening of the race both physically and morally unless the trend is reversed or stopped.

The eighteenth and nineteenth centuries, with the rapid growth of industrial cities built at great speed and with poor housing conditions, led to the anti-urbanists becoming even more vocal, as they now had concrete evidence of the vices of the city. The high crime rates of the city and the physical deterioration of the population as shown by the poor physique of city recruits for the army provided the evidence to stimulate the growing tide of anti-urbanism. The inevitability of urbanism by the end of the nineteenth century meant that the twentieth-century writers had to re-evaluate city life. It was here to stay and so it had to be made more acceptable, it had to be improved. Thus the criticism shifts to a concern to reduce the isolation of the individual within the potentially anonymous urban structure, to provide the individual with a protection against the advance of conformity, of mass living which the city, with its standardization of work, living and leisure, was seen to produce. The solution to this trend was seen in the creation within the city of 'communities', small social groupings within a particular neighbourhood, areas of the city which would provide primary social relations for the individual to maintain his individuality and, through the neighbourhood community, allow the group to express its individuality within the city so that each area would be somewhat different from the next. This desire can be seen as one to recreate the village within the town, because of the virtues of the primary social relations which could only be experienced in the village setting. It led to what could be described as 'the community centre movement' within British town planning and urban study. During the inter-war and, more particularly, in the post-war period of reconstruction and slum clearance with the development of many new housing estates this question of planning for the community came to the fore in both town planning and urban sociology. Associated with this movement was the idea of the 'neighbourhood unit' which was essentially a planning unit consisting of a certain range of facilities which were required for any population such as schools, shops, play spaces, etc. The idea, however, was developed particularly in the post-war period to include the notion of *social balance*, of not only having an allocation of the physical requirements of the community but also the social and to provide a population which was a reflection of the population as a whole. This desire for social balance grew out of a dislike for the large one-class housing estates of the inter-war period and a belief that the togetherness and lack of social barriers exhibited during the war years should be incorporated in the post-war reconstructed society. The new neighbourhoods to be planned should, according to this theory, be made up of all the social groups in the population in their proper proportions to achieve a social balance. The failure, however, to translate this ideal into practice has been complete. Where elaborate attempts were made in the initial planning to create balance by providing housing for different social groups the balance produced was extremely short-lived and the area reverted to a one-class pattern.

Urban sociology in the inter-war period was very much concerned with the problems of urban development, and in examining the solutions adopted by planners. This led sociologists to concentrate in their studies on the development, or lack of it, of community life on new housing estates, and the lack of success of schemes for socially balanced neighbourhoods. The community centre was found in nearly all of these studies to enjoy a high level of initial success during the early settling-down period of the estate, when the residents were faced with common problems relating to their houses and the provision, or, more likely, the lack of provision, of facilities on the new estates. In most cases the situation was a question of 'antagonism from without breeds association from within'[3] and once this antagonism had diminished or disappeared, the internal cohesion gradually diminished and the population tended to move away from the community-based activities and back to those based on the family. There are still many policy makers and planners who, despite the past failures of the community centre movement, are still strong supporters of the community ideal, as a means of improving the quality of urban life. The arguments that have been traced with their underlying and continuing anti-urbanism are still very much part of contemporary social ideology. To the past city–rural controversy has been added that of the conflict between the city and the suburb and the suburb and rural life which arose during the nineteenth century and has flourished in the twentieth century. The argument about the strength and weaknesses of urban life still goes on, however, but now there has been added the further complication of suburban life.

Clark,[4] writing about the suburban community in Canada, claims that the whole debate about the virtues and vices of a particular territorial way of life has now been switched completely, so that it is now the city rather than the rural area that is the repository of all virtue and the suburb has now been cast in the role vacated by the city of the promoter of an inferior way of life. The suburb is portrayed in terms of a producer of conformity, which makes a thing of 'togetherness', which has burgeoning organizations in which people participate largely to keep up with the rest of the population. Status striving and the drive for social achievement have become the keynotes of the community. This picture is graphically drawn in John Keats's *The Crack in the Picture Window* where he says in his introduction, writing about the United States: 'Developments [in housing] are creating stratified societies of singular monotony in a nation whose triumph to date has depended on its lack of a stratified society, on the diversity of its individuals.'[5] While some of the premises of this statement are clearly arguable, e.g. the fact that America was an unstratified society prior to the arrival of the suburb, it does indicate the kind of belief surrounding the suburb and the kind of consequence which is seen to follow from its development. The attacks upon the suburb have been often of a particularly venomous nature and have often been sadly misinformed about the actual facts and conditions of urban living, preferring to rely on the more impressionistic and unreliable accounts like Keats's book than on a careful investigation of the suburb itself. Thomas Ktsanes and Leonard Reissman summarize the position well when they say:

Sociological literature [on the suburb] is openly vituperative and pejorative in tone. It is a rare piece that finds some warmth and sincerity, or happiness in suburban life. The rest are dominated by judgements of unrelieved damnation. The suburbanite is doomed to remain imprisoned in his box house and in the conforming mould set by his neighbour.[6]

and

suburbs are seen as homogeneous, and undesirably so – the houses look alike, the people think alike . . . suburbia is overwhelmingly a middle-class environment.[6]

This view of the suburb is contrasted with the city, which is now seen in a much more favourable light, as an environment which produces and preserves greater individualism and a 'higher' cultural content.

The suburbs have not always been strongly condemned. At first, they were greeted by some writers with cautious optimism. Low and Weber, who were both concerned with the origins and growth of the suburbs in the nineteenth century, looked to them as the answer to the current urban problem of overcrowding. For example, Low, writing in 1890 of the rise of the suburbs in England, sees them as the possible saviour of urban man who is now able to move out of the insanitary, crowded, unhealthy conditions of the urban environment to one which although not truly rural, is, at least, part rural and part urban. The new suburban man who results is seen as at least the equal, if not the superior, of the countryman in physique and general ability. Weber, writing in 1900, echoes this view, considering the growth of the suburb to be beneficial. He writes: 'The rise of the suburbs it is which furnishes the solid basis of a hope that the evils of city life, so far as they result from overcrowding, may be in large part, removed.'[7] As well as those who looked for physical improvement in the standard of living of the inhabitants of the suburbs, there were those who looked to the suburb to provide a new way of life.

This early hopeful honeymoon period did not last long, however, and it gave way to the period of criticism and attack which now characterizes much of the writing on the suburb. Lewis Mumford, for example, in his book *The City in History* writes: 'The universal suburb is almost as much of a nightmare, humanly speaking, as a universal megalopolis, yet it is towards their proliferating nonentity that our present random and misdirected urban growth has been steadily tending.'[8] What led to this change of view, this growing revulsion against the suburb, which was hailed with such promise? Perhaps one of the reasons is that the suburb failed to produce the 'new civilization', the way of life which earlier writers hoped it would. In fact, it seems to them to have reproduced much of what they wanted to remove from the old. Another reason is advanced by Scott Donaldson in his recent work *The Suburban Myth*, in which he says: 'Intellectuals [in the United States] turned upon the suburbs, where once they had attacked the city for robbing America of its agrarian dream, now they zeroed in on the suburbs, which had betrayed their fondest hopes for a 20th century restoration of the Jeffersonian ideal.'[9] In other words, it was the failure of the suburbs to reproduce the rural ideal.

Not all contemporary writers have adopted such a critical view of the suburbs. Riesman,[10] for example, writing of developments in America, finds something of value in the new way of life in the suburbs. He sees them as providing a link between the urban and rural ways of living. Riesman's concern is not with the physical health of the population but with the broader question of the type and quality of life. Concerning suburbia, he says: 'The American ethos which revolved about the dialectic of pure country versus wicked but exciting city, seems to me now aerated by the suburban outlook. This produces a homogenization of both city and country, but without full integration.'

One man whose thinking about urban development has had a profound effect throughout the world had a very unintended effect upon the growth of the suburb. This was Ebenezer

Howard.[11] Howard was anxious to avoid the formless spread of towns into endless suburbia and his means for doing this was to create new independent communities. Howard's vision was of new towns which would be planned as a whole and would incorporate the best features of both rural and urban living. This would provide an opportunity for a change in human life, a release from the insanitary cities and the limitations of purely rural life. Howard wrote: 'Town and Country must be married and out of this joyous union will spring a new hope, a new life and a new civilisation.' And later, it was to be 'a marriage of town and country, of rustic health and sanity and activity of urban knowledge and urban technical facility, urban political co-operation'.[12]

The Garden City, then, was to be a completely new urban form to be created according to this new principle of Howard's and would lead to the improvement of the human condition. Howard was not just a visionary but was also a man of action and initiated the first Garden City at Letchworth. Letchworth as well as being the first Garden City had a consequence unforeseen and certainly unintended by Howard. Unwin the chief architect of Letchworth and also the chief influence upon the Tudor Walters[13] housing report of 1918 laid down in both cases the standard pattern of housing densities which was to lead to the proliferation of suburbs in the inter-war period. Letchworth played perhaps the most conspicuous part in demonstrating the popularity of the single family house and garden at a density of twelve to the acre which became the norm of the inter-war suburban building. This was certainly neither Howard's nor Unwin's intention as both were firm opponents of the suburb. Perhaps what was even worse than this has been the adoption by the anti-urban segments of society of Howard's ideas to justify the development of the pale apology of the Garden City which is called the Garden Suburb. It was this travesty of Howard's idea which became popular during the wars and his pioneer attempts to create Garden Cities along new and revolutionary lines which found support from only a small minority. The development of these two ideas of the 'garden suburb' and the 'garden city', the latter becoming the basis for the idea of new towns, has continued to be important in tracing the growth of the suburbs and the rationale given for that growth in the post-war period up to the present day. The idea of creating new towns was first given serious national consideration in the 1940 Barlow Report[14] and eventually emerged as one of the means by which London's post-war growth should be tackled in the Abercrombie plan for London. The first New Towns Act was in 1946 and this designated fourteen new towns.[15] The desire to build these towns was motivated by the twin desires of preventing further suburban sprawl and creating a better environment. The first new town begun under the Act was at Stevenage. These however, were the only new towns to be designated until the early 1960s when another set of new towns was begun. In the 1950s the government relied upon local authority and private development which for the most part has resulted in further suburban housing estates usually built to what is loosely described as 'garden suburb' principles which means relatively low-density housing with suitable garden and playing areas which is a far cry from Howard's total conception of the new urban environment. Each of Howard's many proposals which he intended together to form the new Garden City had its own separate band of supporters which has meant that his ideas have been lifted out of their original contexts and used to support developments which Howard was concerned to prevent. For example, there grew up a movement concerned with the preservation of the countryside who adopted Howard's idea of the prevention of ribbon development and the control of urban growth, but were unwilling to give up the kind of amounts of land needed for the development of Garden Cities or new towns. The idea of Howard and his followers which has had the greatest unintended effect has of course been the idea of lower building densities as this was the major stimulus to the growth of the one thing Howard most wanted to prevent, the suburb.

Thus the suburb has its admirers and its critics, those who see it as a link, as a mixture of town and country which can be a viable community in which the advantages of both rural and urban living can be combined, and those who see it as a dull middle landscape which seems to combine all the worst features of rural and urban living.

2 Rural, Urban and Suburban

The simplest distinction which can be drawn between urban and rural is that based upon administrative boundaries. For example, the Registrar-General defines *urban* and *rural* for the purpose of the census as follows: 'urban areas include all urban boroughs and urban districts defined by the Local Government Acts, whereas rural districts are the administrative rural districts defined by the same act'.[1] This definition of 'rural' and 'urban' in terms of administrative areas is entirely arbitrary and does not allow for the changes which have occurred in the composition of the population, particularly of the rural districts, e.g. the growth of new and overspill settlements in the rural districts around the major cities. The Registrar-General also distinguishes areas according to their size, using the following categories: conurbations defined (following C. B. Fawcett) as:

> A conurbation is an area occupied by a series of dwellings, factories and other buildings, harbours and docks, urban parks and playing fields etc., which are not separated from each other by rural land, though in many cases in this country such an urban area includes enclosures of rural land which is still in agricultural occupation.[2]

other urban areas: in this category there are three divisions into urban areas of over 100,000 population, 50,000–100,000 population and under 50,000 population.

The same kind of statistical, administrative definition is provided in America by their Standard Metropolitan Areas.*

* A Standard Metropolitan Area is defined in terms of one or more contiguous counties, has one central city of 50,000 or above and may include other cities within the metropolitan area. In 1950 in the United States of America there were 168 Standard Metropolitan Areas defined by the Federal Bureau of Statistics containing 84,500,680 which was over 50 per cent of the then population of the USA.

Neither of these definitions make any provision for distinguishing the suburb. Suburbs do not have explicit administrative boundaries, they can be part of either urban or rural areas. Also, they do not fit conveniently into any particular size category. Definitions based on administrative boundaries or size categories are only of limited use in the elaboration of the way of life of the inhabitants. Rural–urban comparisons based primarily upon statistical data, usually drawn from censuses, have been used by Lupri,[3] Mann[4] and Moser and Scott.[5] Lupri, in work on West Germany and the United States has shown that although differences are declining they still have some significance. Lupri examined rural–urban differences with respect to fertility, family structure, economics, social and attitudinal characteristics (including here education, measured in terms of the numbers of years spent in school, newspapers read, politics, holidays taken, the possession of certain consumer durables, e.g. television, telephone, etc.) and, lastly, the number of children, if any. On the basis of these comparisons, Lupri considers that rural–urban differences are still crucial to the understanding of 'rural' and 'urban' society. Work on rural–urban comparisons in Britain has not been very extensive. Two studies of note are those of Mann and Moser and Scott. Mann compared urban and rural areas, defined by the Registrar-General, using data drawn from the 1951 census and the Registrar-General's statistical review. From his comparison of population structure, health statistics, vital and social statistics (including marriage, divorce, education and voting behaviour), he concludes that the differences in population structure (age/sex) are still to be found but that his other comparisons show differences which are too slight to be significant or are non-existent. The most extensive study of urban areas based upon census data is that by Moser and Scott. They clearly demonstrate the diversity of British towns, dispelling any illusions that may have been harboured that there is only one type of urban dweller, living one particular pattern of urban life which could be said to constitute 'the urban way of life'.

Where would the suburb be placed in such comparisons of rural and urban? Can it be seen to be similar to the rural population structure or is it nearer to the urban, is it an in-between situation or does it represent an entirely distinct set of characteristics demographically and socially? Of the three studies mentioned, only that of Moser and Scott deals with the question of the suburbs and their variations from the urban or rural area. This study is concerned with the variation of 157 towns on fifty variables grouped under the headings of population change, households and housing, economic character, social class, voting, health and education. Forty-nine of the towns are considered to be suburban, but the criteria for this definition are not made explicit. Taking the forty-nine towns from the total and then comparing the total with the 108 remaining towns, they find that on eighteen of the variables there is no change, and on many others the change is only very slight. However, on two variables, population change (increase and decrease) over the period between the censuses of 1931 and 1951 and job ratio, the change was considerable. This would seem to indicate that suburban towns have increased their population more rapidly between 1931 and 1951 than the non-suburban towns and that suburban towns have a greater daily outflow of people to work in other areas than they have going in to work in the suburban town. The differences in rate of population growth are perhaps related to the defining criteria used by Moser and Scott for the suburb, implicitly if not explicitly. The second factor, that of job ratio, is suggested by them as a means of measuring the extent to which an area is suburban and hence is not used by them as a defining criterion.

In their opening chapter, Moser and Scott say 'One is all too ready to speak of *the* urban dweller, *the* urban pattern, *the* urban way of life without appreciating the variations found both within and between the cities.'[6] Definitions based upon administrative boundaries and studies using the available census statistics have been able to go some way towards demonstrating the variations both within urban areas and between urban, rural and suburban areas, although comparisons with the latter have been very limited due to the lack of any administrative boundary for the suburb. However, the work has not taken us very far in the exploration of the question of how the demographic variations are blended or not into different ways of life. In order to gain insight into this it is necessary to go beyond the statistical comparisons and turn to the work of urban sociologists and social anthropologists who have attempted to explore the distinctive character of rural, urban and suburban ways of life.

Rural and Urban Ideal types

The concern with 'ways of life' has centred on attempts to construct and examine contrasting ideal types of rural and urban living to which have been added the 'suburban' type in more recent discussions. The result of this has been the rural–urban, or folk–urban, continuum which has had a long history within urban sociology, and despite the showers of criticism it has received, it still continues to be the basic model adopted by many urban sociologists for their analysis of society.

Some variant or other on the general theme of rural–urban continuum has been used by, among others, Becker,[7] Durkheim,[8] Maine,[9] Tönnies[10] and Redfield.[11] As an indication of its continuing popularity the most recent elaboration of it is that of Frankenburg[12] in his work on communities in Britain. In this study he develops what he terms a morphological continuum, which is another variant on the rural–urban continuum. A valuable point to begin is that of Redfield whose work, perhaps more than any other, typifies this kind of approach. Redfield sees the rural–folk society as made up of relatively small groups of people who know each other well and who share sustained primary, face to face interactions. Kinship and family networks are extremely strong. Understanding this type of society demands a careful analysis of the kinship system. The individuals in this kind of a society are seen to have similar tastes and interests which are intimately connected with life within the community and have a strong feeling of group solidarity. They are, in the polar type, illiterate and this, combined with the inward-looking orientation, tends to limit the number of contacts that they have with people from outside their own particular locality, consequently their contact with urban life is minimal. Their behaviour is fixed by convention and tradition, the leaders and the positions which people hold within the village are known and moreover, they tend to be perpetuated from one generation to the next. Relationships between the population are on a personal 'total' basis, with the people coming to know each other as total personalities. The control of activities in the society is informal in nature, with conformity to the accepted codes of behaviour being enforced mainly by informal means such as gossip, ostracism and ridicule. The pattern, then, of the folk–rural society is that of the homogeneous, small scale, inward-looking society based upon and bound up with a particular locality.

The picture of urban life finds its most famous exposition in Wirth's essay on 'Urbanism as a way of life'.[13] Wirth's picture of urban life is based upon a series of deductions which begin with the belief that urban life has three principal characteristics. These are that it involves increasing size, increasing density and increasing heterogeneity. The increase in size in the urban area over the rural society results in the individual having many more possible contacts, but, at the same time, this increase in choice limits the depth of contact which it is possible for the individual to have, hence the urban dweller forms secondary and somewhat superficial relationships rather than primary relationships. These secondary relations are based on a shared situation, e.g. work, housing or a shared interest, e.g. religious, political, recreational and tend to be limited to that shared situation, e.g. work based relations not often overlapping with neighbourhood relations. This limitation in the depth of knowledge that is gained by the people of each other in the urban area leads to what Wirth terms 'segmental relationships'. This inevitably leads to an increase in the superficiality and anonymity of urban life which is one of the chief criticisms levelled at the city way of life. It is from the rather impressionistic and purely deductive writings of Wirth and others that this particular image of the city dweller arises rather than from empirical study of the city dweller to discover what is his actual as opposed to his supposed way of life. According to Wirth, increase in size also results in greater spatial segregation within the urban population and area according to ethnic heritage, social class, etc. Whereas, within the rural village all groups lived within a stone's throw of each other, within the city each social and ethnic group carves out its own area and tends to live within it. This is seen by Wirth to be breaking down the overall sense of community and belonging which was characteristic of the rural folk society. This leads again to an increase in anonymity and to a compartmentalization within urban living. The increase in density of the population necessitates changes in the types of social control mechanisms which can be used. The informal controls of the rural society are replaced by formal controls, by the police and courts. The increase in density also brings about a greater standardization of conditions in housing and services. Lastly, the increased heterogeneity of the population which is itself a consequence of the changes in size and density, leads to greater standardization of goods and services. This further encourages the development towards anonymity and segmentalism within the urban population.

Urban society and way of life is seen, then, in contrast to that of the rural, as heterogeneous, with a much greater range and diversity of occupations and voluntary associations (e.g. religious denominations, clubs and societies, theatres and cinemas, etc.). Work is detached from the home environment, the basis of social contacts is widened and contacts become secondary in character. Social control mechanisms are seen to develop to replace the informal controls of the rural society. These then are the two contrasting ideal types of rural and urban which have coloured much of the thinking and work on urban and rural society.

Criticisms of the Rural–Urban Continuum

This approach of the urban–rural continuum can be criticized on a number of grounds. In a society where rural–urban distinctiveness has declined to the extent that it is extremely difficult, if not impossible, to identify any areas which correspond to the two extremes of the continuum, the continued use of it would seem misleading. The earlier discussion in this chapter would seem to indicate that this could well be the case in Britain, in that very few rural–urban differences of any magnitude were found in the characteristics studied. The continued use of this continuum in such circumstances would necessitate fitting data into an inappropriate frame and so prevent the development of new and more appropriate frameworks. Associated with this particular criticism is the fact that the use of the continuum has led in some instances to the neglect of wider changes taking place within the society, changes which may well be of considerable importance in interpreting change in the 'rural' parts of the society.

The continuum has also come in for criticism on the grounds that although it is called a continuum, in practice it has amounted to little more than a dichotomy. The two ends of the continuum have been adequately defined but what of the stages along the continuum from the 'rural' to the 'urban' poles? How are these to be identified and measured? This criticism is one concerned not with the fundamental validity of the concept but merely the failure of its advocates and users to introduce precision into its use. If the rural–urban continuum is an acceptable framework then it is quite possible to suggest a number of stages which might be established, stages which are of importance in examining the changes within both urban and rural society. One such stage would be the commuter village, which is small in size, where face to face interaction and informal social control would be possible but which is not homogeneous, where the population does not share a common basis of work or tradition as part of the population has lived all its life within the village and another part is made up of 'newcomers' to the village. In this situation there are found not only primary, face to face relations, but also quasi-primary relations and secondary. The commuter village hence would represent a case which is neither 'urban' or 'rural' but a combination of both and, depending on the strength within the commuter village of 'rural' and 'urban' elements it could be placed towards one or other pole on the continuum. Another case which demonstrates the necessity for stages to be established along the continuum if it is to be of any value is the 'urban village'. This is the particular kind of community studied by Young and Willmot in Bethnal Green[14] and by Gans[15] in Boston's West End. These 'villages' are communities within the city which do not conform to the general picture of urban life presented by Wirth and others. These are areas with close family and kinship links, with some degree of occupational homogeneity; in the case of Bethnal Green this was work in the London Docks. They are areas of strong informal social controls and a strong locality or neighbourhood identification similar to many rural villages. However, they do have some variation in their occupational base and it would not be possible to live the whole of one's life within these 'urban villages', having no knowledge at all of the surrounding urban society and its contrasting behaviour. The rural–urban continuum does not make provision for these communities which are neither rural nor urban, nor does it make provision for perhaps the most frequent case of a part rural, part urban community, the suburb. However, the whole validity of this approach and the establishment of the categories in between does depend very much on whether or not the continuum is the most useful method of conceptualizing and analysing rural and urban change.

The final line of criticism which is of some importance is that which has attacked the continuum and its proponents for having within it values which are implicitly in favour of the rural. The writing of Wirth, for example, implies that the rural society was inherently more satisfying because it was the scene of complete relationships which endured over a long time whereas the urban was a place of transitory, secondary and segmental relationships which led to anonymity and to a poor quality of life for the individual. The intrusion of the writers' own values and preferences for rural rather than urban living have been considerable largely because of the emotional commitment that many of them had to a particular way of life. These values tended to be an explicit favouring of the countryside because of rustic virtues or else commitment to creating within the urban area communities which were deliberately aimed at producing the advantages of rural living, the primary relationships to find expression through the local community and neighbourhood unit which then act as a counter to the increased anonymity and fluidity of urban living.

Rural and Urban in Contemporary Britain

Some of the difficulties of developing and using the rural–urban continuum as the basis for the analysis of different ways of life found in towns and villages can be illustrated by examining the existence as separate entities of rural and urban in contemporary Britain. The growth in industrial and urban development within society has led to the growing interchange between the city and the village, the urban and the folk–rural. This process has been somewhat awkwardly called 'rubanization' by American sociologists.[16] This growing interdependence is seen to arise from improved transport facilities, the de-centralization of industry, the increasing mechanization of agriculture and the growth of residential suburbs. These processes are leading to a decline in the traditional rural population and an increase in the rural non-agricultural population. These changes are demonstrated in British rural community studies which have a growing concern with the inter-connection of rural and urban life. British rural community studies have been strongly influenced, since their beginning, by the work of social anthropologists and have, until recently, been almost entirely conducted by them. This has resulted in the approach and methodology being based usually on participant observation, with the investigator spending anything from six months upwards within the chosen community. The first study of a British rural community using the anthropological approach as distinct from an historical approach is generally agreed to be that by Arensberg and Kimball[17] who studied family and community in Southern Ireland. This was followed by studies in Wales,[18] Cumberland[19] and Devon.[20] These studies all share a concern to delineate and examine the distinctive character of the rural community. This led to the villages chosen for study being of a particular type. Firstly, they were semi-isolated in upland areas of the British Isles, at some distance from any major urban centre. Secondly, they were all villages which depended very largely upon agriculture as the chief source of employment, with the occupied population being composed very largely of farmers and farm workers. Thirdly, they were relatively small in size, varying between 500 and 700 population. Fourthly, in all the villages the population was undergoing a slow but progressive decline, due very largely to the changing demands of agriculture for labour. In this they were characteristic of most rural areas in this country which are still heavily dependent upon agriculture as the main source of employment. Lastly, a large proportion of their population was either born in the village and had spent all of their life within it or came from within a ten mile radius of it and had moved into the village. Most of the movement into the village had been short distance movement from the surrounding areas. The increasing mechanization of agriculture has led to the decline in the demand for labour on the farm and the consequent rise of non-agricultural employment in rural areas which in turn has produced a growth in the level of economic differentiation within the village. Coupled with this change is the growing volume of migration of urban populations outward to the village and vice versa. These changes have resulted in the earlier type of community study becoming increasingly less valuable as the villagers now recognize and acknowledge comparative reference groups which are not limited to other members of their village. This means that the wider context within which the villagers are living must be considered. It is not sufficient merely to examine the local village community. The shift in emphasis in rural community studies is beginning to make itself felt in the study of Gosforth by W. H. Williams, and has become even clearer in the study of Westrigg by Littlejohn.[21] In the latter study the concern with the rural community is broadened to a consideration of the process by which members of the community are drawn into a wider network of relationships which extends far beyond the local village, bringing them increasingly into a greater contact with the non-rural population. This greater level of contact leads them to compare their status and circumstances with those of the urban situation. According to Littlejohn, such a change brings with it an increase in the importance of class as one of the major distinguishing features. For example, Littlejohn considers that in Westrigg: 'Class is, for its members, one of the major horizons of all social experience, an area in which most experience is defined.'[22] If this is so, then the study of class structure and class relationships becomes important in understanding this kind of 'rural society'. Does this then indicate the intrusion of urban variables or societal variables? This raises the question of the influence of place variables such as urban–rural as against the influence of other variables such as social class. Here at any rate, Littlejohn is suggesting that social class has to be seen as of at least equal importance with place variables in explaining the emerging pattern of life in this particular community. Social class is now seen to provide the key to the understanding of the individual's network of social relations, with the higher his class the more dispersed his network and the lower the class the more concentrated.

The growing interest in the interchange of rural and urban has led to studies of Lowland Britain, of areas within the sphere of influence of the large urban centres. Such areas have been termed 'mentally urbanized rural areas'. These studies have also highlighted the influence of class variables in bringing about a re-alignment of the village social structure. For example, Pahl, on the basis of his study of Hertfordshire commuter villages considers that 'when new mobile managerial and professional commuters move into a village, they live in a completely different social and physical world from the village working class, and this has the effect of polarizing the community on class lines, replacing the traditional hierarchical structure.'[23] This same kind of polarization has not always occurred in the same way as in Hertfordshire, the variations depending on the character of the existing rural population.[24] In these more recent rural community studies both internal and external variables have to be considered in order to be able to explain the way of life found within them.

The change in emphasis which has been traced through rural community studies leads us to see the rural village community rather less as an area in which the individual spends the whole of his life or finds all of his friends and leisure-time activities and more as an area in which he spends only a part of his time. This means that these villages, and this would cover the great majority in Britain, have moved a considerable distance away from Redfield's folk–rural society. They are no longer the isolated, settled communities supplying all the needs of their inhabitants; they are now only supplying some of their needs and at least some of their population have developed characteristics which are ostensibly 'urban' rather than 'rural'.

These changes in rural society (i.e. the total population of a rural place) have led to what could quite well be called the eclipse of rural society in that rural society has ceased to exist as a separate and distinct entity. The traditional rural order of the squire, parson and schoolmaster has broken down through changes in the employment pattern in the rural area and through rural–urban and urban–rural migration. These same changes have led to the replacement of the traditional order by a new order of middle-class professional and business families – the inhabitants of suburbia; the replacement of the distinctive rural society by the half-town, half-country suburban environment.

Suburban Ideal Types

Just as in the rural–urban continuum ideal types of rural and urban were constructed, so attempts have been made to construct an ideal type for the 'suburban'. The best known of these is 'Suburbanism as a way of life' by S. F. Fava.[25] She distinguishes between suburbanism as an ecological phenomenon and as a social psychological state. The former distinction is based upon such characteristics as population size, density and land values and the latter on such things as the extent of neighbouring, rationality and impersonality. In her attempt to create the ideal type of the suburban way of life, Fava first considers the ecological traits which have been demonstrated in studies of the suburbs. There are three of these: first, that the suburbs have a disproportionately high number of young married couples with children. This means that these families are likely to give a prominent place to child-rearing activities. The second feature is that they are largely middle-class in status. The third is that suburbs have certain distinctive physical qualities; they are largely areas of houses newly built by private developers for owner-occupation, with a low density of building and almost entirely composed of residential development. The social-psychological characteristics are more difficult to determine but Fava is in no doubt that 'suburbanism is a "way of life" as well as an ecological phenomenon'. The attribute which is singled out to demonstrate this is that of neighbouring. Within suburban areas there is found to be a high degree of neighbouring which is in contrast to the anonymity and lack of neighbourhood and neighbour relations within the urban area. The suburb, therefore, is similar to the ideal type rural area as it has integrated primary groups. The groups are, however, based upon neighbours which thus replace kin in the suburb, in contrast to the village where kinsfolk form the basis of the individual's social relationships. The way of life which Fava portrays for the American suburb is one which is half-way house between the rural and urban ideal types and could be seen as a third type.

Definitions of the Suburb

Having considered at some length the question of urban, rural and suburban as ways of life and the changes in society which have produced a move towards the half-urban, half-rural environment, it is now necessary to define more closely the suburb. First we must examine the range of definitions which have been offered by previous investigators. Some of these definitions have been based solely on locational grounds. Wissink, for example, says: 'the suburb is a community usually, but not necessarily, incorporated outside the administrative or [central city], but within the agglomeration as a whole'.[26] However, this definition is much too loose and generalized to be of any great analytical value. Another example is that definition put forward by Schärer in a study of Zurich. He defines the suburb as a 'non-contiguous urban development within a non-closed-in open space'.[27] This again is not a definition which is particularly helpful in identifying all suburbs as some areas which have other suburban characteristics are contiguous with urban development. This is, in fact, implied by Wissink when he says the suburb will be 'within the agglomeration as a whole'.

Moving away from the purely locational definitions of the suburb there are those who have suggested additional variables to complement location. For example, Fava uses both occupation and location and suggests as a working definition, 'an area outside of the legal limits of the city but within commuting distance'.[28] She also elaborates this definition by saying that suburbs 'refer particularly to the residential or dormitory variety, characterised by dependence on the city occupationally and for various specialised types of shopping and recreation'.[29] This takes the specification one stage further and sets out in more detail the kinds of derivative characteristics of location which are explicitly suburban. W. Martin[30] also argues along the same lines and elaborates both definitive characteristics of the suburbs, which he sees as its ecological position and the fact of commuting, and derivative characteristics which he sees as demographic and socio-economic factors. The ecological position of the suburb is that of a residential area outside the city but dependent on it as a source of goods and services, and differs in its ecological position from both the rural and urban. The second definitive character is that of commuting and this is seen as a direct result of its ecological position. The first derivative characteristic is that, because it is a residential area there tends to be a preponderance of married couples with children, leading to a particular demographic structure in the suburbs. The second derivative characteristic, like the first, is dependent upon the fact that suburbs are residential areas in which the inhabitants are house buyers, hence suburbs attract the middle income households, the middle class and again give to the suburbs a particular socio-economic character. The same view as that of Martin is expressed, though not as fully, by Dyos[31] where he defines a suburb as a decentralized part of a city with which it is inseparably linked by certain socio-economic ties. The most composite definition of the suburb which combines location, occupation, land use and legal status is that provided by Kurtz and Eicher. Their summary definition of the suburb is:

> location beyond the limits of the legal city (possibly contiguous) with a consistent nonfarm, residential pattern of land use. The residents are primarily employed in urban occupations, mostly in the central city. The area may either be incorporated or unincorporated, depending upon the type of suburb under investigation. However, some municipal services are provided even in the unincorporated suburbs; this is a responsibility assumed by real estate interests. Population growth may be taking place on the periphery and density ratios are intermediate between urban and fringe.[32]

All these definitions so far considered are concerned with the suburb as an ecological phenomenon rather than as a sociological or social psychological phenomenon. They all stress the fact that a suburb is a particular geographical location, which necessitates the inhabitants' travelling to work, which is located in the urban centre. In terms of their demographic characteristics they have a preponderance of young married couples, with children, who are buying their own homes. In order to identify suburbs ecologically indices of the proportion of residential to non-residential land use, extent of commuting and demographic indices of the age, sex and marital status of the population can be used. However, the 'suburban way of life' which this kind of location is supposed to engender cannot be defined in terms of indices and statistics and consequently the definitions are vague and imprecise. For example, Dyos says that in sociological terms the suburbs may be regarded as providing the environment for the satisfaction of many needs of the family and containing some facilities for leisure pursuits. This obviously leaves a lot to be desired as there is virtually no specification at all within the definition; for example, what particular needs of the family are supposed to be satisfied by the suburbs? The most successful way of dealing with the question of the 'suburban way of life' is to explore how living in an ecologically defined suburb affects or does not, the principal activities of the individual, looking here for how work is affected by commuting and for effects on leisure activities and family life. From this kind of analysis it would perhaps be possible to draw up an ideal type of the suburban way of life which could be used for definitional and comparative purposes. As yet such an ideal type does not exist.

The last term which requires brief consideration is that of 'suburbanization'. As with the term suburb, this has been variously described. The concept has been ill-defined because of the ambiguities involved in the term 'suburb'. However, given that suburbs are capable of being defined ecologically as a particular type of residential area, then suburbanization is the process within society which gives rise to this kind of development. Contained within this concept, therefore, are both the wider changes discussed in this chapter, regarding the changing nature of rural and urban and also more particular changes which have given rise to specific suburbs.

The analysis of the suburb will now proceed along two parallel courses. The first will be concerned with the question of the growth development and present position of the suburbs as particular ecological phenomena. The second will be concerned with the rather less tangible but potentially more interesting question of the growth and development of a 'suburban way of life', the extent to which such a phenomenon exists and its relationship to the 'urban life'. This will necessitate being concerned with both the rise of evidence to support a suburban way of life – actual changes in the pattern of behaviour and attitudes of people living in the suburbs – and the rise of the belief that suburbs produce a different way of life: the growth in the 'ideology of the suburban man', an ideology which, as Chapter 1 showed has been the subject of much controversy, not all of which has been particularly well informed and has borne more resemblance to a 'myth of suburban man' than it has to the objective reality of suburban life.

3 The Origin and Growth of the Suburb

The origin of the suburb, like that of the city itself, is far from clear. It is virtually impossible to say at what date the suburb was first developed around a city. However, there are a number of significant points in the development at which the suburb changed in its functions and increased its rate of development. The most significant of these is the mid-Victorian period which heralded the *mass suburb* which has become the dominant form in the twentieth century.

Pre-Nineteenth-century Suburban Development

The suburb seems to have been present even in the earliest cities for which information is available. For example, archaeological findings have demonstrated the existence of a 'Greater Ur' at a distance of up to four miles from the city.[1] There is also evidence that the early Egyptian cities had areas of 'suburban' villas at some distance from the city centre. The suburb from the eleventh to the eighteenth century developed in two directions. One was as a home for merchants and traders, often immigrants, and the other was of the villa dwellings of the wealthy city dwellers. Economic historians[2] have noted the influence in the thirteenth and fourteenth centuries of competition between the city or town residents and those living in the suburbs or in small towns or villages. These suburban dwellers were able to acquire the skills of the city dweller but paid lower taxes and had lower food prices and wage levels. They were also free from the restrictions of the Guilds which operated so powerfully in the medieval cities. London presents a good example of the development of these two types of suburb. Dyos[3] considers that as early as the tenth century the suburbs south of the Thames began with the opening of the first London Bridge. The motives for movement out to the suburbs were mixed, but one powerful factor was the operation of the Guild in the city. In the second half of the fifteenth century the Guild regulations led to the movement out into the suburbs of those whom Clapham[4] terms 'yeomen' i.e. second rank persons of some importance but below a full member of a guild. In the suburbs they could start up a business on their own account though they had not been admitted as a master by the various guilds (e.g. goldsmiths, tailors, cloth makers etc.). They were able to do this in the suburbs because these areas were beyond the jurisdiction of the municipal authorities and the writ of the 'Twelve Great Companies'. Also the suburbs were a place where a man debarred from working or trading in the city might set up his own business. This was particularly the case with foreigners such as the Huguenot refugees, mainly silk weavers who came and settled in the suburbs of South and East London after the revocation of the Edict of Nantes in 1685. Hence the suburbs which developed immediately south of the river, for example, Southwark, were areas of minor industries and trades along with inns and amusements. Together with the activities of the Guild leading people to move out was the increasing cost of land and rents in the City of London which, particularly by the sixteenth and seventeenth centuries, was having a fairly sizeable effect upon the growth of the suburbs of South London. There also developed areas of cheap housing for the urban poor. These took the form of, for example, tenement buildings of high density in Southwark in the sixteenth century. Suburbs of this type that developed were often crowded and unhealthy places, possibly even more so than the City of London itself, particularly as they were left largely untouched by the Great Fire. Suburbs of a different type, the country house type, also existed in the sixteenth century. Sir George Clark[5] in his *Wealth of England 1456–1760* considers that many of the substantial traders and professional men in the sixteenth century combined a career in a city company or corporation with 'their mansions and suburban gardens'. This second type of suburb, hence, was the preserve of the upper class and was situated at a greater distance from the City of London.

This type of suburb increased steadily in importance as the eighteenth and nineteenth centuries progressed, with the cities increasingly being regarded as undesirable places to live in by the higher income groups. This move to the suburbs was given further impetus and rationale by the Romantic Movement which extolled the virtues of the countryman and countryside in sharp contrast to the wickedness and vice of the city dwellers. The development of the more select suburbs was limited for a long time by the lack of transport facilities. The only people who could afford this kind of living were those who could commute by carriage. However, developments in communications in the eighteenth and nineteenth centuries led to a gradual widening of the economic base of the suburb. Dyos's study of the growth of South London's suburbs shows clearly how growth was related to improved communications. He considers that the eighteenth century marked the beginning of the suburban development of South London, as by this time new houses were appearing in the villages of the area. The impetus to the growth was given by the increasing population of London and the development of new roads and bridges in the second half of the eighteenth century. This improvement in communications was continued in the nineteenth century when, after the Napoleonic Wars, three further bridges with connecting roads were constructed over the Thames and this led to renewed residential expansion in the area. As these areas grew so the transport provisions changed, from the hackney carriage to the stage coach to the omnibus, the latter having the most profound effect. It did not appear on the scene until 1829 but was then quickly successful due to the lower cost of travel and the more frequent stops which it provided. During the eighteenth century the suburb was increasingly becoming an exclusive residential area for the higher income groups of the population. This was widened in the nineteenth century as transport provision improved, reducing the cost of travel and the mass suburb emerged.

Five factors were of importance in determining the shape and rate of growth of the modern mass suburb. These are first, the increased mobility of the population arising principally from the improvements in the system of transport; second, the congestion of the cities and the differential buildings by public authorities and private developers, the latter aided by the growth of the building societies; third, the differential availability of land for building; fourth, the development of Town and Country Planning which in the twentieth century has played an increasingly important role in determining the courses of suburban expansion by designating which areas may be expanded and by how much; lastly, the engendering of social aspirations which associated the idea of the suburb with respectability, a high status and an essentially middle-class way of life. These processes taken together have resulted in the modern pattern of suburban development.

The Growth of London's Suburbs

In order to see how each of these processes contributed to suburban growth it is necessary to examine in the first place, the growth of London's suburbs, as they are much better documented, and then to see how far the same processes were at work in the suburban development of other major cities. During the second half of the nineteenth century the population of London's outer ring grew by approximately 50 per cent in each of the ten year periods between the census of 1861 and that of 1891 and by 45 per cent during the period between 1891 and 1901. In the latter period the areas of England with the fastest rates of population growth were all suburbs of London. The growth of the suburb in the second half of the nineteenth century in London was almost entirely the product of the improved system of public transport which allowed commuting to take place relatively cheaply over longer distances. The first omnibus was introduced in 1829 and was immediately successful and by 1834 there were over a hundred omnibus services to South London alone.

The next development in the transport system was the railway. In 1836 the first line was opened between London and Greenwich. This had an immediate effect on the omnibus, forcing the original omnibus owner out of business because of falling receipts. Despite this early setback, the omnibus later re-established itself as an important means of suburban travel. The Metropolitan Railway, established in 1863, further developed local passenger services and then was further expanded by the construction of the first underground line in 1890. Local passenger services were again increased in importance as a means of urban commuting when special workmen's fares were introduced which provided the workers with cheap transport into the centre from the suburbs. The cheap fares were first offered on a voluntary basis, for example, the Metropolitan Railway Company offered them to workers travelling on the early morning train in 1864. However, in 1883 the Cheap Trains Act was passed which compelled railway companies to offer workmen's fares as and when required by the Board of Trade and the Act also repealed the passenger duty on all penny-a-mile fares. This latter measure also had the effect of reducing the cost of commuting. The Cheap Trains Act was deliberately designed and passed to promote the movement out of the centre of London into the suburbs by the working class as one means of easing the problem of overcrowding in housing conditions within the central area of the city. In fact, the Act did not achieve anything like this result due partly to the limited extent to which the various companies did provide cheap fares. The company which did the most in this respect was the Great Eastern and this could be one of the reasons for the spread of working-class housing in this direction from the centre.

The developments in rail transport which facilitated commuting were supported after 1860 not only by the omnibus but also by the horse tram, which was electrified in 1901. After this trams were considerably more successful than the omnibus which was motorized in 1909. Therefore, in the second half of the nineteenth century, there were three principal innovations on the urban transport scene, the omnibus, the tram and the underground. There is some controversy among social historians as to which of these had the most crucial role in the development of the suburbs. The controversy has revolved around the role of the railways. For example, Asa Briggs writing on the development of the Victorian city says: 'The building of the local and suburban railway lines helped to determine the main lines of suburban growth.'[6] This position which gives the key role in promoting growth to the railways has recently been questioned in a study of the impact of the railways upon the development of the Victorian city. The question raised in this study is whether or not the railways developed in anticipation of demand or merely followed rather reluctantly behind the initial expansion of outlying areas. Kellet says:

> The crux of the matter is the question as to whether the railways pursued a policy of cheap suburban fares in anticipation of demand. If this were so, if it could be shown that it was, in fact, systematic policy and regular practice of the railway companies serving London, then there would be some justification for describing the railways as an important cause of suburban growth in the period up to 1900.[7]

Kellet, from his study, considers that there is insufficient evidence to support this view. In London the railways did adapt their activities somewhat to commuting, although these varied from company to company. In the other cities the distance from the new suburbs to the centre were too short to make rail commuting an economic proposition. Even in London, two passengers commuted by horse omnibus or tram for every one by rail. Kellet estimates that there were about 250,000 daily commuters by rail in the London area by 1900, out of a total population of 6½ million, which was probably quite a sizeable proportion of the actual working population of the city. This total was, as noted above, drawn unevenly from the regions with the Eastern having the highest proportion of cheap fare traffic and the Northern the lowest in 1897. It would seem, therefore, that the railways made their greatest contribution by making possible long-distance commuting to areas which could consequently still preserve their exclusive character as upper-middle-class areas. By the end of the nineteenth century long-distance commuting had not reached very great proportions but it did provide the basis for the spread of the population further afield in the twentieth century as the areas nearer to the centre became filled up with residential development and at this stage the railways came into their own as a means of commuting. At this stage they do become of crucial importance in determining the main lines of development but this took place more in the early twentieth century than in the nineteenth.

The growth of London's suburbs has continued and blossomed in the twentieth century.[8] It was still closely associated with the improvement in communications and the development of methods of transport, although there were other factors of importance emerging such as the availability of mortgage funds for house purchase and the distributing of industry which, during the century, has become decentralized. In the suburbs which developed in the first half of the century, the development of new rail and underground links and the improvement of existing services played an influential role in determining which areas developed and at what rate. Some of these developments were the linking of the Bakerloo line to an existing railway line to provide a through service to Watford in 1917, the extension of the Northern line to Edgware in 1924 and the Piccadilly line to Cockfosters in 1933. There were also a number of improvements in existing services to promote more rapid commuting, one of the most significant of these being the electrification of the Southern Railway in the 1920s. There was also the continued expansion and improvement in the bus and tram services which also facilitated commuting. As the century developed it became increasingly apparent that the motor car would become a factor in suburban development hence the improvement of the road system began to assume greater importance. The development of the North Circular Road and Western Avenue in the 1920s are important because they led to a new pattern of commuting, from suburb to suburb around the edge of London rather than from suburb to the centre of the city. This latter type of commuting has increasingly come to be the preserve of the middle and lower middle class.

Suburban development since the last war has been accompanied by a large rise in car ownership making the residents much less dependent upon public transport. An indication of this can be found in a traffic survey conducted in 1962 which shows that in the inter-war suburbs at least 30 per cent of the households possessed a motor car, whereas, in the outer, post-war suburbs it was 45 per cent.[9] The importance of the car as a vehicle of commuting has increased in the 1960s with the growth taking place in many areas around the major cities which are not accessible without a car and many new housing estates are planned explicitly for the car-owning family.

The provision of housing during this period is also a factor in conditioning the type of suburban development which took place. The bulk of the houses constructed in the inter-war period were constructed by private builders. This is particularly true of the period after 1932 when changes in government subsidies to local authorities led to a virtual halt in local authority building. In the period 1919–32 the London County Council obtained sites outside the then boundaries of London and developed 'cottage' estates of various sizes and so contributed quite substantially to suburban expansion, particularly eastwards into Essex. The largest of these 'cottage' estates, built at Becontree in Essex for 112,000 people, was completed in 1932. The population of these 'cottage' estates was working-class, hence they represent something of a new type of suburb and can be seen in contrast to the middle-class private suburbs and the older 'faubourg' type working-class suburbs of the medieval city, and sixteenth- and seventeenth-century London. The housing built over the same period by the private developers was, until about 1930, almost entirely for middle-class occupation as they were the only group likely to possess the necessary 25 per cent deposit. However, after 1930 the credit position improved, making it easier to buy houses with a low deposit, as little as 5 per cent in some cases, hence owner-occupation spread to the lower middle classes. The 1930s were characterized, therefore, by the development of private housing estates of small three bedroomed semi-detached houses which were aimed at the young married middle- and lower-middle-class couple with one or two children. By 1939 this had led to an area up to fifteen miles from the centre of London being pretty well entirely covered by housing at a density of somewhere around twelve to fourteen houses to the acre.

During the inter-war period an important influence upon the house building market and, therefore, upon the growth of the suburbs, was the growth of owner-occupation promoted by the emergence of the building societies as an important financial institution. The provision of cheap finance contributed very largely to the boom in house building in the 1930s in a time when most other sections of the economy were badly depressed. The first building society was established in Birmingham in 1781 but it was not until 1846 that the first building society of the modern type was developed and not until 1874 and 1894 that the societies were given a statutory basis. The twentieth century saw the growing influence of building societies as their assets expanded. The characteristic feature of the growth of the societies was that it was a movement of small societies giving small advances. For example, by 1930 over 75 per cent of the building societies (just over 1000 in total) had assets of less than £100,000 and only 1 per cent had assets of £5,000,000.[10] During the early part of the century the advances given by the building societies were 'to help working men become home owners' and 51 per cent of all advances were of less than £500. In the inter-war period the assets of the building societies expanded as, in a time of general economic uncertainty, they were an attractive investment. This expansion enabled the societies to finance house purchase. Until 1930 the loans were usually only up to 75–80 per cent of the purchase price, consequently this limited the buying of new houses particularly to the upper income groups. After 1932, however, interest rates were at their lowest and this, together with arrangements like the Builders' Pool whereby the builder would deposit a sum of money with the building society as a security against 95 per cent advances to people buying his houses, enabled particularly the lower middle class to buy houses. The spread of home-ownership through the occupational structure was quite considerable. In 1932, for example, the borrowers of one society, the Abbey Road, were 37 per cent wage earners, 24 per cent salaried employees, 19 per cent independent workers, farmers and professionals and 20 per cent were in miscellaneous occupations.[11] Without the financial provisions of the building societies the suburban expansion of the twentieth century both before and after the war would have been very much more restricted. Hence, in the twentieth century it is not possible to look solely at transport provisions and improvements as the main or only stimulus to suburban expansion.

The variations between the private and public building noted for the inter-war period has continued in the post-war years. During the period 1951–8 the house building done in central areas of London, mainly in connexion with slum clearance schemes, was done almost entirely by local authorities, private builders contributing only 8 per cent. In the outer suburban areas however, the position is reversed, with the private builders responsible for over half the total houses built. Since 1958, there have been signs of change with the private builders' share of the central market rising from 8 per cent to nearly 33 per cent, but this building is mainly expensive, exclusive flat construction for the wealthier sections of the population.

A further factor which has had a continuing influence upon the course of development of the suburbs, which has received rather less attention than transport but which is probably as important if not more important, is that of land ownership values and availability. Even before the rise of the modern suburb of the nineteenth century, land ownership and availability played an important role in determining the pattern of city growth. It was the lack of land and its high price in the city which led the poor and the traders to move out of the city to find accommodation which was cheaper. This led to the growth of the South London suburbs of the sixteenth and seventeenth centuries noted earlier. With the improvement in communications between South London and the City in the eighteenth century, the local landowners on the south side began to change their land holdings to allow for building development. Prior to this the large estates had covenants which explicitly prevented them from building, leasing or selling their land for building. The majority of the landowners in South London, according to Dyos's study, did convert their leases from 1770 onwards to building leases with the express purpose of 'projected improvements by the erection of substantial buildings'.[12] Development in this area took place, therefore, on the estates which had been converted, some of the owners resisting the move towards building development until much later. The growth of the suburb in the nineteenth century was similarly influenced by the shortage of land in the cities which stimulated outward expansion and the availability of the land on the edges of the cities, conditioned by the landowners' readiness to sell and let their land for building purposes. The land shortage in the cities has grown more severe in the twentieth century where increasingly the city authority has had to buy land outside its boundaries for its surplus and rehoused population, for example, the cottage estates of the London County Council in, for example, Essex and Surrey. Land ownership also affected the development of the transport system, as again the railways could only develop where they could obtain land for their track and stations. Kellet, in his study of the role of the railways in the nineteenth century, places great importance on the role of the land market and the attitudes of the landowners. He writes: 'The closer and more detailed the study, the more important become the attitudes and decisions of local landowners, builders and established residents, and the less readily does the mere establishment of a rail linkage seem to provide the dramatic explanation of the course of suburban growth.'[13] Further evidence on the role of land availability and ownership and its influence in determining the price of property has been demonstrated in a number of studies. For example, there is the study of Radlett in Hertfordshire by Coppock[14] which shows how the local landowners have played a large part in determining the rate and direction of the expansion of the area. Another recent study of the housing market has shown how the movement of population to suburban areas takes place out of sheer necessity, the suburb being the only place where the people can afford to buy a house, rather than out of any positive desire for suburban living, in response to rising or changing social aspirations.[15]

Town and country planning has increased in importance as the twentieth century has developed. The first legislation on town planning was in 1909. This act can be seen to have grown out of the nineteenth-century concern for and legislation about health and housing conditions. This original piece of legislation was revised after the First World War in 1919. The Act required all boroughs and urban districts over 20,000 to prepare plans for their areas. The Act set a time limit for this task of seven years. However, this was first extended and finally abolished in the Town Planning Act of 1932. The next landmark in the progress to full control over town development was the Barlow Commission and Report published in 1940.[16] The commission was set up to examine the whole question of planning and the extent of state and local authority control. The commission as a whole recommended a more active role for central government in planning and a minority report advocated the establishment of a separate ministry for town and country planning, the latter being adopted in 1943. This was soon followed by the Act of 1947 which brought practically all development under local authority and state control by making development subject to planning permission. The same Act transferred planning from the district councils to the county boroughs and the county councils. This very brief review of the growth of town planning legislation shows that by 1947 quite extensive powers existed to control and direct residential growth, hence all post-war suburban expansion has been affected in some respects by planning controls. In the immediate post-war period planners were committed to the view that the growth of the large cities should be restricted. This is well illustrated by the Abercrombie Plan,[17] published in 1945, upon which the post-war development of London has been based. The plan divided London into four concentric rings for planning purposes. These were the inner ring, which was an area of densely built up housing, mostly in need of renewal. The plan estimated that to rehouse this population in reasonable density and allow for the provision of parks, roads, etc., in the redeveloped inner ring would require the overspill of one million. The second region was that of the inter-war suburbs. These had a fairly static population and were expected to continue to be stable, with, if anything, some slight decline. The third area was the green belt, which was to expand by only 125,000. In fact, this area has grown by more than 300,000 with the development of new housing estates. Fourthly, came the outer region, which was to accommodate the bulk of the overspill in new towns and expanded towns. The increases in employment in the London area, together with natural increases larger than expected, coupled with the slowness with which new towns have been developed have seriously distorted Abercrombie's figures and estimates of growth, which were soon reached and exceeded. For example, projected figures of population for 1971 were reached by 1961. The growth of London's newest suburbs in the post-war period, in the outer region rather than in the green belt, was determined by the overall plan for the London area, hence suburban development has become less haphazard and more related to the availability of land with planning permission than to the availability of public transport services, although these are still of importance in determining which towns in the South East have expanded and will expand most rapidly in the future, as the population of London moves yet further out in search of space.

The changes discussed in the transport system in the nineteenth century encouraged the working class to move out of the congested centre of the cities and these same changes also encouraged the middle class to move still further out from the existing suburbs into which the working class were moving. Hence, it is possible to see a constant outward movement of the population, with the middle class moving even further outwards as the working class pushes out from the centre into areas which were formerly middle-class residential areas. There are many examples of this kind of movement documented, with respect to the growth of late-nineteenth-century London. One study by D. A. Reeder,[18] shows how in Acton during the first half of the nineteenth century the area remained largely unaffected by new developments but after 1861 the village turned into a middle-class residential suburb. With the boom in suburban development after 1883 the area experienced a major building boom in low cost housing and, by 1913, the area was 'overstocked with low cost housing',[19] and had taken on a broadly working-class appearance. The former middle-class residents had begun to move or had moved further afield. Other areas, for example, Ealing until 1921, were rather more successful in maintaining their middle-class character and preventing low-cost housing development. Another change which has occurred within formerly middle-class or upper middle-class residential suburbs is quite well illustrated by the case of Paddington. Paddington became an early- and mid-Victorian suburb, and at this time, was firmly part of upper middle-class London, but towards the end of the Victorian period and later it began to develop symptoms of physical deterioration. The large houses of the Victorians were taken over by commercial concerns, turned into flats and in the most recent times taken over for multiple occupation by various immigrant groups. All these factors combined have led to the decline of the area's social status and desirability, and this decline began with the movement out, towards the end of the Victorian period, by the middle-class families who had created it. A similar trend has also occurred in other similar areas of London.

Towards the end of the nineteenth century the working class, through the changed transport system, were able to move out from the centre into the suburbs which were begun by the middle class. The image which these suburbs held was, therefore, largely a middle-class one. This meant that a move to the suburb was seen as a requirement of the working-class man who desired to be socially mobile. The working-class man who had heightened social aspirations was the one most anxious to take up suburban residence. The suburb did not hold this image for the whole of the Victorian period but rather it was seen to develop strongly as the age progressed and suburbia developed around the major cities. In the early part of the Victorian era, some suburbs were not superior residential areas. These were the suburbs around some of the industrial cities which conformed to the 'faubourgs' associated with the medieval city, where the workers who were unable to afford to live within the city had their residences. These suburbs were often overcrowded and unhealthy and as undesirable as the congested central city areas. These 'faubourg' type suburbs can thus be seen in sharp contrast to the middle-class residential suburb with its low density housing and with the incorporation of garden city principles into its design, which came to typify the suburban development of the late nineteenth and twentieth centuries. These early industrial suburbs can also be seen in contrast to the late Victorian suburbs built by the philanthropists for their workers in part as social experiments and in part to provide healthier living conditions for their workers.

The relationship of the move to the suburbs with heightened social aspirations has aided the development of the 'suburban way of life' which is closely related to, if not synonymous with, a middle-class life style. Dyos,[20] writing of Camberwell in London, considers that attempts to define the suburb are rather like attempts to define the middle class who created it. The presence of status distinctions within the suburb has led to each area having a distinctiveness. This has been taken to considerable lengths in many cases. For example, Dyos, in his study of Camberwell, found that the type of house, layout of gardens and types of trees planted in the roads denoted different levels of social class: limes and horse chestnuts were the mark of the well-to-do, whereas acacias and laburnums were for the middle incomes and unadorned macadam was for the wage earners. The importance of the house and garden as a reflection of social rank has often been quoted by those who have studied twentieth-century suburbs. The suburbs then reflected and still reflect a changed pattern of living from that found within the central city areas.

Ruth Glass,[21] discussing the development and prospects for the future sees a return to urban living and aspirations away from the suburban. This trend is seen in the desire to renew and redevelop the central areas of the city with housing as well as commercial developments so that the city no longer has a 'dead heart'. The possibility of such a redirection of population exists but as yet little concrete evidence is available to show that it is occurring. The problems lying in the path of such a redistribution of population are considerable. One that is perhaps crucial is that of the 'Anglo-Saxon sentiment for greenery and a tradition of single family living' which remain strong, and are features difficult to reproduce in the centre of the city where the developments are often in the form of multi-storey dwellings. This desire for a contact with nature for one foot in *rus* and one in *urbs* has been in many ways the mainspring of the suburban image which has given rise to the expansion of residence into the countryside around the cities, spreading further out as the areas become more densely built up.

Growth of Suburbs around selected English Cities

The growth of the suburbs around the major cities of England in the nineteenth century followed a similar pattern to that of the London area, the initial impetus to development of the suburbs coming from improvement in the system of public transport which allowed a greater volume of commuting to take place over longer distances at a lower cost. The important development in the transport system of cities outside London which seems to have stimulated suburban growth more than any other was the horse omnibus rather than the railways. In order to see this development, the growth of the suburbs of Birmingham, Manchester and Leeds will be considered.

In Birmingham the development of the suburbs depended at first, as in London, upon the private carriage, hence they were the preserve of the wealthiest sections of the population. However, this was modified when the first omnibus connected the inner suburbs to the centre of the city in 1834. The number of such omnibuses steadily increased after this date throughout the rest of the century. Commuting was further facilitated by the development of the trams after 1872. Until 1871 there were no suburban railways in Birmingham and its area largely because the distance from the centre to the suburbs was not very great and so rail transport was uneconomic. By 1874 the first set of inner suburbs was becoming entirely built up and a new set was being developed at a greater distance – three to four miles – from the centre. In 1871 the first suburban railway was opened, the Birmingham and West suburban railway. This was followed by the Harborne railway built in 1874. One of the most interesting suburban developments in Birmingham in the nineteenth century was Edgbaston which was a carefully planned residential estate which became the home of many of the influential families of Birmingham during this period. Although the area was only one mile from the centre, it retained its exclusive suburban character throughout the century. In the early twentieth century the railways were a means of commuting for only a minority of the population and the period 1903–14 was one of falling receipts for the suburban stations opened in the last quarter of the nineteenth century.

Another example which shows a somewhat similar pattern of suburban growth is Manchester. It grew very rapidly in the nineteenth century as an industrial and commercial centre and with this expansion came, increasingly as the century progressed, a large number of people, particularly middle-class, migrating from the city to escape the congestion, dirt and other attendant evils of the city and to enjoy the purer air of the countryside. This movement was apparent in the first quarter of the century although at that time the movement of the population was not very sizeable and depended upon private carriages rather than public transport. Even so, migrants commuted considerable distances from places in Cheshire such as Alderley Edge and Wilmslow. As the century developed Manchester grew in size so that by 1831 it was 142,000 and with the growth in the size of the city came the growth of the suburbs, which changed from the home of the select few to a situation in 1920 when it could be said that the whole population were 'looking for a place in the suburbs'. Again, the significant development, as in Birmingham, was the growth of improved transport facilities. The first omnibus was instituted in 1824 and after that date services showed a steady expansion. The growth of Manchester as a trading and commercial centre led to the rapid development of large areas in the centre with warehouses which created further pressure for the outward movement by using up land and forcing rehousing. One writer, commenting upon this at the time, wrote: 'The increasing business of the town is rapidly converting all the principal dwelling houses, centrally situated, into mercantile establishments and is driving most of the respectable inhabitants into the suburbs.'[22] Again, in Manchester, as in Birmingham, the railways seem to have played a relatively minor role in the development of the nineteenth-century suburbs. In the 1840s there was the development of one suburban line, a branch line of the Manchester South Junction railway which was opened to Altrincham. Apart from this there was little interest shown in commuting traffic by the railway companies. In the 1880s a pressure group similar to the one which led the campaign for the Cheap Trains Act in London, was set up to press for cheap fares for the working class to enable them to leave the city for the healthier, less congested suburban areas. Little was in fact achieved and by the end of the century fares were still too high to allow working-class commuting. Hence, Manchester in the nineteenth century became increasingly left to the working class with the wealthier sections of the population moving out to the new suburban areas to the north and, particularly, to the south of the city. This movement has further expanded in the twentieth century. In the growth of the suburbs in Manchester in the nineteenth century the factors which were important were improved transport facilities, the increasing size and congestion of the city, the demands for space and land by the commercial and industrial concerns of the city and the desire of the movers to live in a pleasanter country surrounding, away from the squalor and filth of the industrial city.

The final example is that of Leeds as this again was a city which experienced rapid growth and industrial development in the nineteenth century rising to 172,258 by the middle of the century. A similar pattern to that found in Birmingham and Manchester is exhibited, with the suburbs receiving their initial impetus with the development of the horse omnibus, although the beginning of the movement is somewhat later. In 1858 there were five omnibuses daily leaving the centre of the city for the suburbs which Asa Briggs notes were areas of 'prosperity and opulence'[23] in contrast to the industrial suburbs which developed to the south of the city at Hunslet and Holbeck. These latter suburbs had more in common with the faubourgs of the medieval city and the suburbs of South London in the sixteenth and seventeenth centuries than with the more usual middle-class suburbs of the nineteenth century. The tram appeared in 1871 and further stimulated the growth of the suburban ring. Once again the role of the railways was very minor.

Unlike the London area, rail travel never assumed very great importance, with commuting by train being reserved in all cases for the few and these the wealthiest sections of the population. The lack of rail commuting is due principally to the shorter distances between the suburbs and the city centres which made the alternative forms of commuting travel very much cheaper. The railway companies were even less interested than they were in London in fostering commuting, being much more concerned with the far more lucrative inter-city travel. The other factor of importance in all of the provincial cities discussed was the flight from the city of the wealthier groups which gave the suburbs their appeal to the rest of the population as areas of high social status, and led to their being seen as possessing a way of life to which one should aspire.

In the twentieth century the expansion of suburbs around the provincial cities has shown even greater and more rapid growth. In order to see something of this, six of the major cities of England have been chosen. They are distributed across the country. They are Birmingham, Bristol, Leeds, Manchester, Nottingham and Newcastle. The analysis of their growth will involve first a consideration of the developments of the cities themselves compared to their hinterlands from the 1921 census to the 1966 census estimates and also an examination of the extent of suburbanization in the hinterlands of the cities. This will be measured by the job and commuting ratios devised by Moser and Scott for their study of British towns, based upon the 1951 census.[24] The job ratio measures the proportion of people who move daily into a particular area to work, e.g. Central London has a high job ratio as there are few people who live and work in the area, hence most of the people who work there travel each day. The commuting ratio is a measure of the proportion of people who live in one place but move out of the area to work each day. For an area to be suburban it would require a low job ratio i.e. few people entering the area to work, and a high commuting ratio i.e. the majority of the population leaving the area daily to work elsewhere.

Taking the six cities together then Table I shows that there was a much smaller rise in the population living in the cities than in the surrounding urban and rural districts. The highest rate of growth is found in the rural areas which are the areas which have most recently been drawn into the suburban expansion. However, there are a number of interesting variations among the cities. Two of the cities show a population decline over the period 1921–66. These are Newcastle and Manchester; others have been saved from this by boundary changes and annexations of the growing surrounding areas, for example, Birmingham. Yet, despite annexations, the growth rate of the cities never rises above 16 per cent, reaching nearly 16 per cent in Nottingham and 15 per cent in Birmingham. There is also considerable variation in the growth rates of the hinterlands of the cities. Those with the highest growth rates are Bristol, Birmingham, Nottingham and Manchester (all rates over 114 per cent) and the lowest rates are Newcastle with 45 per cent and Leeds with 12 per cent.

TABLE I

Population Changes in Selected Cities and their Hinterlands

	Total Population			*Size Increases*		*% Increases*	
	1921	*1961*	*1966*	*1921–61*	*1921–66*	*1921–61*	*1921–66*
All cities	2,308,598	2,635,478	2,556,190	326,880	247,592	14·16	10·72
All urban districts	483,565	794,235	835,970	310,670	352,405	61·25	72·82
All rural districts	205,906	403,656	459,390	197,750	253,484	96·04	123·11

Source: Census of Population 1921, 1961, 1966.

County volumes for Cheshire, Durham, Gloucestershire, Lancashire, Northumberland, Nottinghamshire, Somerset, Staffordshire, Warwickshire, Worcestershire, Yorkshire (West Riding).

Bristol emerged as the city with the highest hinterland growth rate, 145 per cent on the 1921 census figure. In the hinterland the growth rates were highest in the rural districts (172 per cent) rather than the urban districts. This was particularly true of those to the north of the city where the suburb of Filton which contains the British Aircraft Corporation works lies outside the city boundaries. Much of the other expansion in the northern part of the city's hinterland is linked with this particular employment centre, with many of the professional, scientific and technical staff living in new developments which have expanded villages in the Thornbury and Sodbury rural districts.

The expansion of Manchester also illustrates the same process of city-hinterland expansion. In the case of Manchester, the expansion has been much greater (173 per cent) to the south of the city in Cheshire, compared to 56 per cent to the north. This pattern has been established since 1921, from which time the Cheshire region of Manchester's hinterland has shown a steady increase in population by 38 per cent in 1921–31, 47 per cent from 1931–51, 22 per cent 1951–61 and by 9 per cent 1961–6. In the Lancashire part of the area, the expansion has been much more modest, with 9 per cent from 1921–31, 33 per cent 1931–51, 6 per cent 1951–61 and 1 per cent from 1961–6. As early as 1921 the city of Manchester needed building land outside the city boundaries and in 1926 purchased the Wythenshawe Estate, some 9 square miles of Cheshire. This area has subsequently been developed to provide housing for 90,000 people and so contributed in no small way to the suburban expansion.[25] The expansion of population in Cheshire since 1921 has been entirely due to the growth of Manchester's suburbs, as the older industrial centres of the area have steadily declined in population over the same period. The suburban expansion has led to the transformation of Cheshire villages and towns, swamping the original and blotting out the old landscape, before the ever-increasing tide of suburbia.

One further example is that of Birmingham. Here one difficulty arises more acutely than in the cases of the other cities in examining population movements over the period. This is the masking of the changes through boundary revision as Birmingham has expanded its boundaries taking in a number of the adjacent local authority areas. Without these changes, there would have been a substantial decline in the city's total population.

As it is, the city's population has remained, throughout the period, at about the million mark. The hinterland growth rate for Birmingham from 1921–66 is around 120 per cent so there is evidence of a considerable population devolution from the centre. In the 1951–61 period Moindrot[26] on the basis of census figures, estimates that 80,000 people left Birmingham, moving out into the peripheral towns and rural areas. The greatest population increases were in the districts adjoining the Birmingham conurbation, particularly the rural districts of Warwick, 33 per cent, Meridon, 51 per cent and Seisdon 70 per cent. Most of these migrants are commuters. Hence, once again, the familiar pattern emerges of the city spreading as the population moves out into the new suburban areas, in search of living space.

To reduce the scale of the analysis of change still further, one area within one city hinterland can be examined to show that variations occur within this general pattern of city expansion. If the Bingham Rural District in Nottinghamshire is taken as an example, variations in growth rate can be demonstrated. This particular rural district lies to the east and south of the city of Nottingham. During the period between the censuses of 1951 and 1966 the area increased in total population from 16,866 to 32,742, an increase of approximately 94 per cent. However, not all of the parishes in the area expanded equally. Out of a total of forty parishes, twenty-two increased in size, thirteen decreased and five remained more or less unchanged. The largest increase occurred in those parishes which lie nearest to the city of Nottingham and here the greatest increase was one of 240 per cent on the 1951 figure by 1966. This parish was one of a number which had large new housing developments which have all but obliterated the original villages. These increases have led to a greater degree of suburbanization as measured on job and commuting ratios. In 1951 the job ratio for the Bingham Rural District was in the lowest category and this remains unchanged in 1966. The commuting ratio, however, changed from the third quartile to the second quartile indicating an increase in the volume of commuting and, therefore, suburbanization.

The six cities were examined using job and commuting ratios to measure the degree of suburbanization of their hinterlands. Moser and Scott examined the same cities in 1951 using the census data of that year to calculate the ratios. Once obtained, these scores were divided into quartiles. The work of Moser and Scott can, therefore, be used as a base upon which the change by the 1966 census can be measured. Table 2 shows the changes in these ratios over the fifteen-year period. Overall, there is evidence of a move towards increased suburbanization. This pattern can be illustrated by examining certain of the cities in more detail. In Birmingham, for example, there were eight rural and urban districts ringing the city for which figures were available for both 1951 and 1966. Those not available were the subject of boundary changes. In 1951, all fell within the lowest quartile on the job ratio index and in 1966 they were all still in this category, hence unchanged in their degree of suburbanization measured in this way. On the commuting index in 1951 seven fell into the second quartile and one in the highest or first quartile, but by 1966 the distribution of the eight areas had changed so that there were now four in each of the first two quartiles. Hence, for three of the districts there had been an increase in their degree of suburbanization.

Taken together, the evidence of population changes and job and commuting ratios does demonstrate the prevailing trends towards city dispersion and an increased degree of suburbanization of the city hinterland, noted earlier for the London area, around the cities examined. This has led to increased commuting and the separation of living and work, even more sharply than had previously existed in the cities, this being one of the most important characteristics of the modern suburb.

From this discussion of the origins and growth of the suburb a number of points stand out clearly as significant factors. The impetus for the development of the *mass suburb* and the shape that this has taken were determined prior to the Second World War very largely by the improvements which took place in communications and the system of public transport. In this context, the important influences were the development of the omnibus and tram, and in the London area the train and the tube. Outside the London area the influence of the railways was minimal,

Table 2

Job and Commuting Ratios

(a) *Job Ratio*

Scores	*1951*	*1966*
0–79 most suburban	50	50
80–99	1	3
100–111	—	—
111+ least suburban	3	1
Total	54	54

Source: Census of Population 1951 and 1966.
Categories based on those used by Moser and Scott.

(b) *Commuting Ratio*

Scores	*1951*	*1966*
0–30 least suburban	4	1
31–51	6	3
52–86	26	23
86+ most suburban	18	27
Total	54	54

Source: Census of Population 1951 and 1966.

and they did not even assume extensive influence in the metropolis until the twentieth century. Other influences upon the development of the suburb in this period were land availability, the growth of easier credit arrangements through the building societies and the development of local authority housing estates in the 1920s. After the Second World War, there were changes in the influences upon the continued growth of the suburbs, with public transport declining in importance as a factor in determining both the rate and shape of growth. The new factor was Town Planning legislation and controls which served to determine the areas where future suburban expansion could take place. The growth of private transport also made longer distance commuting more viable and also introduced a new criterion in the selection of areas for development, the provision of roads rather than the availability of public transport. Throughout the period the role of the building societies as providers of relatively cheap finance has been important as has the factor of land availability.

Suburbs, as they developed, particularly in the eighteenth and nineteenth centuries, changed in their functions. Prior to the development of the *mass suburb*, there were two types, the country house type with villa dwellings of the very wealthy and the faubourg type with dwellings of the urban poor. This position changed in the nineteenth century when the suburbs became increasingly of only one type, areas of middle- and upper-class occupation, the symbol of middle-class respectability and of the goal of rising aspirations by the working class. In the nineteenth century the growth of the middle-class suburb was very much linked to the Romantic view of town and country living, which saw the suburbs as a source of salvation from the dirt and congestion of the city. The suburb was a place of healthier living where the rural virtues could once more be found. This view has persisted into the twentieth century despite the development of the *mass suburb* which bears little resemblance to that envisaged by the early Romantic writers. The suburb in the twentieth century has become larger in scale and more varied in type as the century progresses. There are now suburbs of all shades of social class. The lower-middle-class suburbs developed extensively between the wars in many estates of small semi-detached houses in areas of, for example, Middlesex, and working-class suburbs of a very different type to the faubourgs began to develop in the form of the cottage estates of the local authorities in the 1919–32 period. This proliferation and move away from the upper-middle-class suburb has led some writers, notably Lewis Mumford, to argue that the whole idea of the suburb has now become a grim antithesis of the Romantic idea. Mumford writes:

> In the mass movement into suburban areas a new kind of community was produced, which caricatured both the historic city and the archetypal suburban refuge: a multitude of uniform, unidentifiable houses, lined up inflexibly, at uniform distances, on uniform roads, in a treeless communal waste, inhabitated by people of the same class, the same income, the same age-group . . . Thus the ultimate effect of the suburban escape in our time, is, ironically, a low grade uniform environment from which escape is impossible.[27]

Mumford, however, seems unduly sensitive to the physical structure created, assuming that this inevitably ends the kind of social life which was part of the Romantic suburban ideal and too insensitive to both the manifest and latent feelings of those moving into the suburb. Is it not true that the modern suburban dweller sees the suburb in the same kind of way as the middle-class Romantics of the nineteenth century? This could be the case, although the physical structure of the suburb may have changed. Standardization of housing does not, of necessity, mean standardized people or, of necessity, a loss of the suburban ideal. The popularity of suburban living and the changed physical form do not inevitably produce a way of life which is in any way different from that of the suburbanite of the nineteenth or indeed of any century.

4 The Growth and Development of the Suburbs: United States, France and Japan

The growth of the suburbs has been traced for Britain, but is this a universal phenomenon which has been produced by the same set of factors or is it one which is peculiar to certain countries? In order to clarify this issue the growth of the suburb in other countries will be examined to discover whether or not the same factors are present. The countries examined have been selected because of their cultural differences and different patterns of historical development. The United States, for example, has a relatively short history of urban living with only 3 per cent of the population living in cities at the beginning of the nineteenth century. France and Japan, on the other hand, have both had a long history of urban living but have very considerable cultural differences. France, unlike Britain and America, has had a tradition of relatively dense living in multi-storey dwellings, rather than in single-family houses. The average density of dwellings in Paris is 114 people per acre compared with 43 per acre for London and the highest density found within Paris is 365 people per acre whereas in London it is only 147 per acre.[1] In France, Paris has always exerted a very powerful attraction upon the rest of the country, certainly more so than any one city in the United States and probably more so than either London or Tokyo, the latter only developing in the eighteenth and nineteenth centuries as the major city of the country. Japan has been the most recent of the countries to industrialize and develop its cities, but the pace of its urbanization and the consequences have been dramatic. If then these very different countries are taken as examples, and if they are found to have similar patterns of suburban development, then it would be reasonable to assume that the suburb is not just a feature peculiar to one or two countries but is a developing feature of urbanism in all of the countries of the world.

United States

In the United States the growth of the suburb has been very much more a feature of the twentieth century than of the nineteenth. The nineteenth century in America was principally the century of urban growth, urban concentration and the development of cities. The urban population in the nineteenth century increased eighty-seven times, compared with a population increase for the country as a whole of twelve times.[2] This expansion of the cities was very closely related to the economic growth and development of the nation as a whole. However, despite this general trend towards centralization and city growth there were also signs of what was to be the dominant trend in the twentieth century, the growth of the suburb. In both New York and Boston their respective suburbs were growing faster than the cities towards the end of the nineteenth century. The city of New York, for example, attained its maximum population in 1860. Since then it has shown signs of decline, most of the population leaving the city and finding its new home in the suburbs. This movement of at first only the upper income groups soon developed into a flood and the rate of growth in the twentieth century has risen until somewhere in the region of 50 per cent of the population of the United States now lives in the suburbs. Kirk, commenting on the tremendous growth of the American suburbs in the twentieth century, has written: 'Everywhere we see the growing place of the metropolis and suburbia in our national life ... two generations ago, in 1900, the median American lived in the countryside; by 1930 he lived in a small town of 5,000 or 10,000 population. Today [1960] he lives in a metropolitan area, increasingly in the suburbs.'[3] The beginnings of the suburban movement in the nineteenth century were related, as in Britain, to developments in the system of public transport and to the increasing congestion of the cities which led to the middle class leading the exodus which gradually spread to all other sections of the population as they too began to aspire to a higher social status which inevitably led them to seek a house in the suburbs.

The role of improved transport is again important as this was the stimulus to the development on the city edges. The provision of quick, cheap transport led to the areas becoming an economic proposition for developers. One example of how the system of public transport stimulated suburban growth in the nineteenth century is documented in a study of Boston.[4] In this study, which covers the period 1850–1900 Boston became a metropolis with the old city ringed by suburbs of various types. Before the railway and the tram, the wealthy sections of the city owned two houses, a town house for the week and a country house for the weekend and for holiday times, to retire from the busy and increasingly congested city. The first omnibus was introduced in 1826 but was not a great success, largely due to its slowness and expense. This was followed by the railway in 1835, which, as in many British cities, did not have a marked effect upon commuting as it was too expensive for short trips for all but a few of the wealthiest citizens and often not very convenient. The railway was, therefore, of most value to the wealthy groups, some of which now felt able to give up their town houses and live entirely in the country. It was not until the second part of the nineteenth century that the expansion of the suburbs accelerated with the advent of the tram in 1852. During the remainder of the century the pace of suburbanization rapidly increased until it became something of a mass movement by 1900, by which time the now electrified tram reached out to a distance of six miles from the city hall in Boston. The expansion of the suburbs in the period after 1850 which was stimulated by the tram mainly affected middle income families who still worked in the centre of the city. The suburban development over this period can be divided into three categories, dependent upon the social class of the individual. The first group was the wealthiest upper-class group which accounted for about 5 per cent of the population. This group always lived the furthest distance from the centre and at the lowest densities. For this group the railways provided a cheap means of commuting. They were found between 3½ and 10 miles from the city centre by 1870 and this had increased to between 5 and 15 miles by 1900. The second group is the central middle class which is the group with which the mass suburb is usually associated. They were found from between 2½ and 3½ miles from the centre in 1870 but 3½–6 miles in 1900. For the final group, the lower middle class, the construction of new housing was almost entirely within the old city, infilling towards the perimeter of the city boundaries. By 1900, however, it had moved to a band of between 2½ and 3½ miles from the city centre. This pattern illustrates the way in which the higher social groups have progressively moved further out and have been followed by the lower social class groups in a steady process of city dispersal.

The late nineteenth and twentieth centuries saw the development of improved systems of transport in the cities of the United States. The flood of middle-class people to the suburbs, noted in Boston, became a national phenomenon, although it was not until after 1920 that suburbanization became the common feature of all cities. For the period from 1900–20 Douglass provides figures to show the rate of suburban growth in cities of over 100,000 and in cities of over 200,000.[5] The average rate of increase of the suburbs of both these groups of cities was 29 per cent. However, for the largest cities, this rose to a rate of increase of 32 per cent with the highest rate being in Detroit, with an increase of 225 per cent.[6] The growth of the suburbs from the mid-nineteenth century to 1920 resulted in some 15 per cent of the total population of the United States moving into the suburbs. This suburbanization was not found evenly across the country: the highest rates of suburban growth were found around the cities of the north-eastern region (New England and New York states). The growth rate of the suburbs during the 1930–40 decade was depressed as was the whole of the United States economy, as, unlike Britain, the building industry was affected by the slump, and the new building rate slackened appreciably, creating a backlog of demand which led to the tremendous housing pressure in the post-war period when the suburban boom reached its height. The suburbs gradually increased their distance from the city centre over the period 1900–50, due in part to the development in the 1920s of the motor car which enabled convenient commuting. The motor car together with the extension and modification of the road system were the most important transport changes in the post-1945 period. After the war the public transport system which originally gave impetus to the suburban expansion went into gradual decline. During the period from 1950–60 the suburbs accounted for nearly 97 per cent of the population increase of the 168 standard metropolitan areas. This growth was on the whole greatest in the largest metropolitan areas. For example, in the areas of over three million the growth rate for the cities was 1·7 per cent as against 98 per cent for the suburbs, whereas for those of under 100,000 the figures were 26 per cent for the cities and 74 per cent for the suburbs. Even in the smaller areas, however, suburban growth was substantial. Two factors have served to prevent these figures for suburban as against city growth from being even larger, these being the annexation by the cities of surrounding areas and the movement into the cities of Negro and other low-income groups, which have slowed down the rate at which the cities' total population has declined.[7]

The second influence upon the growth of the suburbs has been the reaction against the increasing congestion of the city and the desire to rediscover the rural ideal in less dense and more attractive living. The fashion for suburban country living with the one-family dwelling was set in both the United States and Britain by the wealthy families and was adopted by the rising middle class in the nineteenth century. This adoption was facilitated and made respectable by the Romantics who flourished on both sides of the Atlantic, extolling the virtues of rural life. The mid-nineteenth century saw the first planned *Romantic suburb* which was the product as much of the businessman as of the Romantic intellectual. The first of these suburbs was Llewellyn Park, developed during the period 1853–69 and was created for businessmen and intellectuals who could afford to live in it. The suburb was connected to New York by rail, hence it was possible to commute to the city. The whole suburb was planned as a 'retreat for man to exercise his own rights and privileges'.[8] This was followed in 1868 by Riverside Park, designed by Olmstead and Vaux,[9] some nine miles from the centre of Chicago. This was planned as a desirable middle-class residential area. The explicitly Romantic period, however, was superseded (towards the end of the century) by the *Domestic suburb* which was much less grandiose and much more functional, with the objective of providing single-family houses for the growing volume of middle- and lower-middle-class people who were moving in ever-increasing numbers from the congested cities.

Once these initial factors, transport and the reaction to congestion, had begun the move to the suburbs, other factors entered in to affect the course of development. The most important of these are the existence of differential housing opportunities in the cities and the suburbs, the demand for housing, and the provision of easier financial help to prospective home owners.

The different rates of population growth between the city and the suburb in the twentieth century have been conditioned, to a large extent, by the housing opportunities available to the population. Just as in Britain, the role of land ownership and availability was crucial in determining where and when expansion outside the city was both possible and economically viable. In the period after 1945 there was a definite shift in the proportion of new housing built within the city and in the suburbs, with increasingly more houses being built in the suburbs. This shift was the product of an absence of suitable building land in the city and the relatively low cost and empty areas of the suburbs. This trend towards increasing amounts of new building in the suburbs has also been partly the result of the failure of the administrative boundaries of the city to change at the same rate as the physical city has expanded. This development of new housing outside the administrative boundaries of the city was also one of the features of the suburban growth of the city hinterland of the British cities.

The second factor which led to the boom in the post-1945 period was the tremendous demand for single-family houses. This demand was the result of a number of conditions. The first was the depression of the 1930s which had led to a falling off of home building which created a housing shortage. This shortage had been solved at the time by an increase in the number of rooming houses which were mostly seen by their occupants as a short-term measure, until they could obtain a house of their own. The second was the demobilization of the American forces following the end of the Second World War. This process was completed by January 1946. These ex-servicemen were all given liberal benefits on demobilization which they could use to facilitate house purchase. Many of these servicemen were also awaiting demobilization and return to civilian life to marry and settle down, hence the next few years saw something of a 'baby boom'. The net effect of the demobilization benefits and the increase in marriage and families together with the lack of housing in the 1930s was to create an unprecedented demand for houses which the house builders sought to meet at great speed by building tract suburbs of standardized houses. Some of these suburbs would appear to have left a lot to be desired in terms of the quality of the housing, if the sad tale of woe which befell John Drone in Keats's *Crack in the Picture Window*[10] is any guide.

A further influence upon the housing market was the steps taken by the Federal Government to facilitate the easier purchase of houses. In 1934 the Federal Housing Administration and the Veterans' Association were established to help provide mortgages for house buyers. The latter was established specifically to help ex-servicemen and was particularly influential in the post-1948 period. During the period from 1950–4, for example, 44 per cent of all houses were started with Federal Housing Administration and Veterans' Association support.[11] Under these two organizations it became possible to buy a house with no deposit, at low rates of interest and with long repayment periods, hence it became in many cases cheaper to buy a house than to rent one. Large-scale building by private builders before the establishment of these organizations was virtually an impossible task, in contrast to Britain where the development of building societies did provide finance for house purchase and hence for the private builder, somewhat earlier, and from other than government sources. In Britain government help came in the form of local authority housing estates for renting by lower income groups, rather than financing of house purchase.

The future trend of the suburbs in the United States, according to a recent report by the Committee for Economic Development, will be for the growth of the suburban population to continue.[12] The report estimates that by 1975 the central city population will have fallen to 42 per cent of the metropolitan total, while the suburban and fringe areas lying outside the city boundaries will have expanded to include 57 per cent of the population of the entire metropolitan complex. However, there are those who detect other signs than this continued expansion of the suburban population; Parrott[13] for example, in an analysis of the growth of the suburbs of New York considered there are signs of a slackening of the flow of population from the city and a beginning of the return of the population to the city. In New York over the period 1950–7 between 1,000,000 and 1,250,000 moved out of the city to the suburbs. This outflow was principally of the middle class, the wealthier elements of the population, which left increasingly only the poorer sections of the population, creating the present problem of many American cities, that of raising the money to pay for the city services. However, the suburbs also have financial problems and in this lies one of the main reasons that Parrott identifies as important in explaining the return of the population to the city. The greater distances and the increased congestion experienced now by the modern commuter have become an important disincentive to suburban living. The most important factor, however, is financial. The suburban exodus was principally by young couples with children, seeking their own homes, hence one of the most important issues in the suburbs is the education of the children, and education is expensive. With the rising cost of local taxes to pay for the new schools and the necessary equipment for them, suburban residence becomes progressively less attractive. This lessening of the attractiveness of the suburb is seen in the trend over the period 1950–60 in new residential construction, which shows an increase in city building, particularly of high-priced apartment buildings which Parrott suggests indicates that the wealthy, the first to move out to the suburbs, are now moving back and that they may be followed by other sections of the community. This return to the city, however, if it is occurring, is as yet at an early stage and for the foreseeable future the suburb will be the dominant urban form.

France

In France, again, the suburb in its modern form is a product of the nineteenth century. There had been suburbs for the wealthy since the Middle Ages around the major cities, particularly Paris, but these had only been small and had contained a very small proportion of the total population. The movement of large numbers of people to the suburb began in the mid-nineteenth century and accelerated rapidly in the twentieth century when the major decentralization of the cities took place. In the nineteenth century, between 1801 and 1881 the population of France grew by 40 per cent but that of the cities grew by considerably more, indicating that this was primarily a period of urban concentration. The cities of 20,000 or more, excluding Paris, grew over this period by 145 per cent, and cities of 100,000 or more, excluding Paris, by 185 per cent. Paris, already by far the largest, grew by 134 per cent in this period and clearly became the dominant city of France.[14] The city of Paris from the beginning of the nineteenth century has increased its area by fifteen times so that today it covers 2·4 per cent of the area of France and contains some 8½ million people within its boundaries. This expansion of Paris has led to the growth of suburban areas. The earliest of these were incorporated into the city in 1859, increasing the city's population by some 500,000 and so maintaining the city's place as the largest city of France. The first major factor for the growth of the suburbs of Paris was the development of the railways in the period after 1856, which created suburbs along the railway lines stretching out of the city. From a study of the eastern suburbs of Paris it is possible to see something of the growth rates of the suburbs during this period. Between 1851–72 some of the suburbs in this study quadrupled (Montreuil 3,810 in 1851; 12,295 in 1872).[15] Others trebled and still others doubled in size. Hence the suburban movement was increasing in scale as the nineteenth century drew to its close. In the period 1872–96 further growth was found in the suburbs of eastern Paris studied: for example, one suburb had 851 population in 1851, 2,380 in 1872 and 5,016 in 1896. Towards the end of the nineteenth century a further factor apart from the the growth of the urban centres and the development of new forms of transport entered on the scene to promote growth in the suburbs. This was industrial decentralization.

In the twentieth century, these factors noted as influential in the nineteenth century all played an important part in further stimulating suburban expansion. Together with the railways, there was the Métro, the bus and the car, all enabling commuting to take place over longer distances, at greater speed. The development of industry in the suburbs played an influential role in the establishment of industrial suburbs to the west, north and south-east of Paris. Turning again to the study of the eastern suburbs of Paris, the growth which began in the nineteenth century continued in the twentieth with dynamic growth taking place in the majority of the communes. In the period 1921–46 it is interesting to note that one of the earliest communes to expand began to decline in population, losing most to another suburb situated further out from the city. With the influence of the various factors distinguished, the inter-war period saw the rapid growth of suburbs of various types, the principal ones being the industrial and the residential. With this expansion came the growth of the commuting population of the city. Some figures for daily commuting from the eastern, principally residential, suburbs to the city give some indication of the size of the commuting population in 1931. St Mur, with a total population of about 48,000, had a commuting population of 9,256.

Between 1946–54 the city of Paris grew by 4 per cent whereas its suburbs grew by rates of from 12 to 21 per cent. This same pattern continued to 1962 during which time the rate of increase in one suburb rose to 35 per cent.[16] This outward growth of the city shows no real sign of slackening at the moment, hence continued suburban growth at the expense of the city can be expected in the remaining part of the present century.

There are a number of features which are common to the development of the suburbs in France, in Britain and in the United States of America. These are the stimulus to the growth of the suburbs by improved transport and the congestion of the city. However, there are a number of differences in the structure of the suburbs of Paris from those of the cities in Britain and the United States. The first of these is the higher density of population in the Paris suburbs where the average is about 31 per acre instead of 12 per acre or even less. This is due to the greater variety of types of accommodation in the Paris suburbs which are not only acres of the universal semi-detached but also incorporate multi-storey flats. Higher densities and multiple dwellings have been very much more part of the culture of the French cities than they have been in either Britain or the United States, where the ideal has always been very strongly that of the single-family dwelling house. The second difference is that the rich, in particular the rich of Paris, do not, according to George,[17] have the same desire to live outside the city. Rather, they live in high-class areas within the city, particularly the west of Paris. Consequently, there are not many suburbs for the rich. The suburbs are predominantly lower-middle and working-class, the latter being the industrial suburbs of the city.

Japan

The third example is Japan, the first of the Asian countries to develop extensive urban industrial structure which despite the considerable cultural differences is not unlike that of western industrial countries. The cities of Japan are not a new phenomenon. Kyoto, for instance, can trace its origins to 794. The growth of the cities began to be significant in the sixteenth and seventeenth centuries when the size of Kyoto rose from 350,000 to 400,000. However, until the middle of the nineteenth century the major proportion of Japan's population growth took place not in the urban but in the rural areas. At the beginning of the nineteenth century Japan had a number of quite well-developed and sizeable cities. Tokyo was to become increasingly dominant in the nineteenth century, and in 1801 had a population of over one million which was greater than both London with 864,000 and Paris with 547,000. City growth began in earnest in the second half of the nineteenth century with industrialization creating jobs which attracted the rural population to the cities. During the period up to 1920, when the first modern census was taken, the proportion of rural migrants to the population of Tokyo was one of forty-seven in every hundred.[18]

The 1920 census provides the basis for examining the tremendous twentieth-century growth of urban Japan. The population of Japan had doubled between 1852 (27·2 million) and 1920 when it was 55 million, and of this rise in population, the cities took an increasing share. For example, Tokyo had trebled in size from just over 1,000,000 at the beginning of the nineteenth century to 3,358,000. This growth in the urban population resulted in just over 18 per cent of the total population living in the cities. In the period from the 1920 census to the war, the growth of the urban areas was very much the growth of the urban cores and the six largest cities grew at the fastest rate (Tokyo, Osaka, Nagoya, Yokohama, Kobe and Kyoto).[19] The war led to a period of stagnation in city growth until 1950 and from then till the present city growth has continued at a fast rate. From 1950–60 Tokyo maintained the fastest growth rate of these six largest cities (20 per cent). This growth was the result of three factors: the continued migration from the rural areas to the urban for work, the natural increase of the city population and the expansion of the city boundaries which led to the incorporation of suburban areas. By 1960 Tokyo had grown to 9½ million out of a population of over 93 million which means that one out of every ten Japanese lives in Tokyo, which is some indication of the way in which Tokyo has come to dominate the rest of the country. The growth in the 1950–60 period was limited to under half the total number of prefectures of Japan, which further emphasizes the way in which the growth is a product of population migration from the rural to the urban areas. From 1960 to the present the same trends have continued with the population rising to over 98,000,000 in 1965. This growth again being in under half the total number of prefectures. Tokyo has also continued to increase, reaching nearly 11,000,000 by 1965. This then is the background of continuing rapid urban growth, which in its early stages was principally directed towards establishing and building up the urban centres, but as the twentieth century has progressed due to the development of improved transport facilities, the congestion of the city and the intervention of the planners to control urban growth, the cities have been moving towards decentralization, with expansion of the city hinterland bringing the familiar pattern of suburban growth. The city of Tokyo is the best example to illustrate this process because it is the largest and best documented. Japanese urban sociologists have distinguished five periods of development of the city and its hinterland. The first period is from 1909–12. This lies at the end of the Meiji era and sees the development of the urban centre of the city. At this stage the development of the cities had not begun. There was still space within the city for both residential and industrial development. In this period, however, there was the development of the railways which were to become much more important as a means of commuting and in determining the lines of future development. The second period is that between 1918–22. During this period heavy and chemical industries developed, making demands upon both space and population. It was during this period that the development of the suburbs began, with both factories and population moving out of the central areas. The third period is 1929–32, when the growth of the suburbs became the dominant feature of the urban area of Tokyo. This movement which began through industrial development creating congestion and reducing living space was further accentuated by the earthquake and great fire which badly affected Tokyo in 1923. This suburban growth of the post-1929 period was greatly assisted by the development of modern rapid communications, the electrification of the railway lines in this period being particularly significant. The fourth period is the one immediately after the war, 1945–8. The destruction once more of central areas led to pressure on the outward growth of Tokyo. The final period began in 1959. From this date onwards Tokyo became characterized by marked urban sprawl, with its associated growth of suburbs and commuting population. It has been estimated that the commuting population of Tokyo is now the largest of any city in the world, with a figure of nearly 30 per cent of the population of the metropolitan area travelling daily to work in the centre. This trend has been accentuated by the gradual concentration since 1955 of the head offices of most of the leading industrial and commercial enterprises in Tokyo which has given rise to a tremendous growth in the number of salaried white-collar employees in the city.[20] Since 1960 the maximum growth rate for the Tokyo area has taken place at a distance of ten to fifteen miles from the city centre.

There has been a tremendous decentralizing process in the twentieth century in Tokyo which has produced a metropolitan area containing the city and a collection of suburbs around its boundaries. The reason for this particular pattern of growth and the influences upon it are by now familiar enough. First there were the improvements in the basic system of public transport, the railway, the bus and the tram, which facilitated the movement of large numbers relatively cheaply. The motor car is now beginning to make its impact and has created further problems of congestion in an already overloaded transport system. For example, one commuter line to one of the western suburbs was on a typical working day at the peak travelling times about 308 per cent overloaded. The second influence upon the pattern of growth was the adoption of planning control. The first instance of town planning in Japan was in 1889 with the publication of regulations for the reorganization of Tokyo. After the war, the Japanese were again presented with a problem of reconstruction, and to tackle the growth of Tokyo they adopted a similar solution to that of the Abercrombie plan for London. The planners considered that the city must be limited in size and separated from other urban areas by a green belt. The population which could not be accommodated in the city was to be moved into new towns created at some distance from the city which could therefore be more than suburbs, possessing a separate identity and occupational structure. The plan for Tokyo consequently envisaged three regions. The first would be a built-up area extending about ten miles from the centre of the city. This would then be the limit of the city and expansion beyond this would be prevented. The second zone was a seven mile wide green belt which was intended to encircle the city and hence hold it in check. The third zone was seventeen to forty-five miles distant from the centre and was to be the area where the new satellite towns were to be developed.[21] This plan, like the one for London, has only had a limited effect in stemming the growth of the metropolis. One consequence has been to lengthen the commuting distance of many of the Tokyo workers. This type of plan cannot work while the city centre is still an expanding centre of employment.

The last influence upon the growth of the suburbs and the

suburban way of life lies again in the connexion of the suburbs with middle-class and higher-income groups. This provides a stimulus to the rest of the socially mobile population to achieve a suburban residence, which is an indication of an improved social position. The way of life of the middle-class, suburban, commuting Tokyoite is the one which, through its portrayal in the mass media, is coming to be accepted as the Japanese way of life. Dore,[22] in his analysis of city life in a ward in Tokyo, shows how the different social groups lived in different districts, the Shitamacha or downtown, which was long established as the home of the non-Samurai merchant and artisan families, and the Yamanote (or hillside), which has traditionally been the district of the town mansions and the feudal nobility. The Yamanote area includes today the professionals, business executives and the clerical workers of Tokyo's offices. The areas of modern Tokyo which are seen as Yamanote districts are the white-collar suburbs, the areas to the west and south-west of the city served by the electric railway lines. The indication that there is still a status distinction between these two areas is that successful merchants move from the downtown areas out to the Yamanote areas which are suburban and join the band of daily commuters. Hence, suburban living is associated with the higher social groups and is increasingly being aspired to by the other groups in Japanese society.

This brief examination of the United States, France and Japan has shown that the development of the suburbs and the consequent spread and decentralization of the city is becoming the predominant characteristic of urban development in the advanced urban, industrial nations of the world. Not only is this true but also there appears to be some considerable evidence to suggest that although there are factors peculiar to each country, there are also factors which occur in each case. The most important of these are the developments in the system of urban transport in the nineteenth and twentieth centuries, the railways and the tram in the nineteenth century and the motor bus and the motor car in the twentieth century. This improved transport system allowed an ever-widening band of the population to join the very wealthiest groups in living further away from the congestion of the city centres. One notable variation is the difference in type and density of the buildings in the suburbs of French cities. Another variation has been in types of plans adopted for city growth and the extent of government intervention, this being the most marked in the case of London and Tokyo where fully developed and almost identical plans were adopted for the limitation of the growth of the city and the creation of new towns to prevent further suburban development in the area immediately adjacent to the city.

5 Types of Suburb

Suburbs are not homogeneous. There are features which they all share and there are common reasons for their growth and present extensive development, but all suburban areas have not developed in exactly the same way. The sources of the differences that exist have been ascribed to three different factors. These are the types of physical development which have produced a particular suburb, the social class of the resident, and the dominant activity of those within the suburb.

The first criterion for distinguishing between suburbs is, then, that of physical development. The simplest distinction which can be drawn here is whether or not the development was planned and controlled. The most common case is the 'estate suburb' which constitutes the majority of the suburbs around the cities of Britain. These are the new housing estates, either private or local authority, which have grown up to provide houses for the expanding city population and to re-house the population either from areas which were destroyed during the last war or from areas of urban renewal. They are characterized by the single-family, semi-detached house. In America this type is known as the 'tract suburb' and is the one which mushroomed in the 1950s with the post-war boom in housing. The planned suburb is the type which gives rise to the 'popular' image of the suburb and suburban man with its standardization of design and layout of the estate both internally and externally. In contrast, in the unplanned suburb, the development of new housing takes place over a period, during which time the village or town is gradually taken over by migrants and the area becomes suburban in character. This type of suburb has been aptly described as the 'reluctant suburb'.[1] It is typified in the commuter village which experiences immigration from the city and eventually becomes dominated by the commuter element within its population. The Exurb,[2] is perhaps another variant which belongs to this category of unplanned suburb. The Exurb is the area of residential development of an expensive and exclusive type, beyond the existing suburbs, in which each house is different in contrast to the standardization of the planned suburb. The features which separate this type from the other unplanned suburbs are its distance from the city and from the city's suburban areas and its high-cost exclusiveness.

The second criterion for distinguishing between suburbs is that of social class. The idea of the suburb has traditionally been very clearly associated with the middle class, with the suburb and suburban life stemming from the middle class. This association of the suburbs with the middle class was strengthened by the virtual absence until recently of studies of working-class suburban areas. The middle class, however, is not a homogeneous category and different studies have demonstrated the existence of a variety of middle-class suburbs. These range from the study of Gans,[3] of lower-middle-class Levittown to that of Whyte's[4] Park Forest which is the home of the young upwardly mobile executives, to that of Crestwood Heights[5] which is composed of substantial independent businessmen and professionals. These variations within the broad category of middle-class could then be distinguished as separate types of suburb except that they all present variations on a common theme, which has been shown to give them greater similarity to each other than any of them has to the working-class suburb. The commonest means of distinguishing a middle-class suburb is on the basis of the occupational composition of the population (i.e. non-manual worker equals middle-class). Attention was drawn to the existence and importance of the working-class suburb by Berger[6] in America and Willmott and Young in Britain.[7] In both cases the studies were of the growth and development of new estates of manual workers.

The third criterion is that of dominant activity. This type of classification has been used quite extensively in the United States as a basis for the construction of suburban typologies. One of the earliest of these was that developed by Douglass.[8] He draws the distinction between residential and industrial suburbs which represent for him the decentralization of consumption and production respectively in the industrial society. Similarly, on the basis of this original distinction he formulates four major types of suburb. These are 'the poor industrial suburb', 'the decentralized residential suburb', 'the well-marked suburban community' and 'the mixed suburb'. It is difficult to see the logic behind these four distinctions. The first type includes both a qualitative distinction regarding its level of income with the question of the degree of industrialization which presumably could be measured quantitatively, and given that a 'poor' industrial suburb is distinguished surely logically there should also be a 'rich' industrial suburb, or are all industrial suburbs in America poor? Also the use of 'well-marked suburban community' as part of the typology is difficult to appreciate as this category makes a reference to the principal defining criteria, 'industry' or 'residence' as the dominant activity. Hence although the original basis for the typology was clear the actual types which result appear to be far from clear. Another attempt at constructing a typology is that of Harris[9] who bases his work on the same kind of distinction and seeks to illustrate the types by reference to the 1940 census. In all, Harris produces five types of suburb.

The first type is an industrial suburb in which there are many factories but relatively few residents. In contrast to most suburbs commuting is, therefore, into the area. The designation of such an area as a *suburb* is perhaps questionable when it does not conform to one of the basic distinguishing features of the suburb. The second type is the industrial/residential suburb. This contains not only factories but also a sizeable resident population who work in the area, hence it is relatively self-sufficient and has little commuting either into or out of the area. This type is heavily dependent upon the city for wholesale, retail and professional services. The third type is the dormitory or residential suburb where industry is relatively insignificant, if not completely absent. The dormitory suburb is also heavily dependent upon the city for the provision of services. The fourth type is the one which is a mixture of the industrial and dormitory, i.e. the mixed suburb, This category is split into two by Harris depending on whether industry or residential areas predominate.

However, by doing this he is making the distinction between this type and the industrial and residential almost non-existent. The fifth type is one where there is a mixture of coal-mining and manufacturing. This choice seems somewhat eccentric and difficult to justify in terms of the underlying logic of the typology. This typology, despite its five types, in fact only distinguishes between residential and industrial suburbs. The four types, excluding the last which appears to have little relation to the others, express the degree to which a particular suburb conforms to one or the other of these two polar types. This typology falls down as did that of Douglass on the same ground – that of failing to make the 'types' mutually exclusive and give clear indicators to measure the characteristic attributes of each type. Without these a typology has little value. A third type of dominant activity suburb is that of the resort or recreational suburb. Some writers would place in this category the seaside towns which developed during the latter half of the nineteenth century, for example, Bournemouth.

A number of the writers on the suburbs have constructed typologies based on more than one criterion. For example, Clark[10] in his discussion of suburban development in Canada produces a typology which is based upon the type of development, which he discusses in terms of type of house, as well as the overall layout, and also dominant activity. Putting these together he produces six types in all. These are first the single family residential development of the 'pure suburban type'. The second is 'the semi-detached residential development of the 'pure suburban type'. The third is the single-family residential development in a built-up area. The fourth is the 'packaged or semi-packaged' residential development. The fifth is the 'cottage-type development', and lastly the residential development of the pure suburban type which is now five to ten years old. This typology, however, is again not of mutually exclusive categories as categories one and two could be the same; after all family residential development of the *pure suburban type*, whatever this might mean, surely could be semi-detached. This same kind of failure to make the categories explicit and clearly distinguishable exists throughout the types. Moreover, it is a contradiction in terms to have within a typology of suburban types a 'pure suburban type'.

The work of Berger in America and of Willmott and Young in Britain has demonstrated that classifications by type of development alone is of limited value as similar types of physical development can produce varied suburban forms depending upon the social class of the residents of the suburb. Willmott,[11] for example, in his study of Becontree comments that the layout of the estate is similar to that of the middle-class areas but the pattern of social life which he found was not identical, and the source of the difference lay in the class composition of the two areas. The planned working-class and the planned middle-class suburb hence share features in common while having significant and important differences. Similarly, the unplanned suburb presents variations when the class composition of the residents is taken into consideration, with the majority of the reluctant suburbs being middle-class in character as this is the group which can afford to buy the houses provided by speculative developments which create this type of suburb. It is also possible to show differences between suburbs with the same dominant activity but with a different social class composition, for example, between the residential middle-class and working-class suburbs. A fourfold typology based on the social class and dominant activity of the suburban dweller has been used by Ashworth,[12] in his analysis of the development of suburbs in Essex and also by Moser and Scott[13] for their classification of suburban towns, although in the case of Moser and Scott the use of social class is at times implicit rather than explicit. By combining therefore two of the three criteria distinguished it is possible to say significantly more about the suburb than was possible by using any one of the criteria on its own.

From this examination of the criteria which have been used as a basis for previous typologies, one point which emerges very clearly is the inadequacy of any one of the existing typologies, or any of the single criteria. On their own neither the type of development, nor the social class, nor the dominant activity can provide an accurate indication of the likely kind of social life and activities which will be found in the various suburbs. A useful typology must incorporate into it the principle of mutually exclusive types which are clearly and easily definable and this the existing ones have failed to do adequately. Typologies which have combined two of the criteria have moved a step closer to obtaining a full and complete perspective, but most of these have still left much to be desired. A much more comprehensive typology is one which combines not just two but all three criteria into one typology which could then be used to systematically categorize all suburban communities along these three crucial dimensions. Such a typology would give eight possible types, ranging from the middle-class, planned residential suburb which is the closest approximation to the popular image of the suburb to the working-class, unplanned industrial suburb which corresponds closely to the idea of the faubourgs of the pre-industrial city. Some of these resulting eight types are more common than others with the majority of the present suburbs accounted for by the first four types. Existing studies of the suburb in Britain and America can be classified within this typology (see Table 3).

The first of the types distinguished is that of the middle-class residential suburb. This type is often seen as the archetype of suburbia, the one which has contributed powerfully to the development of the popular stereotype of the suburb and the suburban way of life. The structure of this type of suburb is the formally laid-out estate or tract suburb, with its long rows of uniformly built and identically (or nearly so) designed semi-detached and occasionally detached houses, with their neat lawns and gardens. According to Young and Willmott the semi-detached house built since 1918 is more than a symbol of the suburb, it is in fact the suburb. The housing estates built by private builders for the increasing numbers of prospective home owners are the most common examples of this type and exist around pretty well all the cities in England and Wales. Their development in Scotland has been much slower and more recent in origin. This type of suburb is characterized by 'the collective attempt to lead a private life' (Mumford)[31] and by the problems of creating new institutions to meet the needs of the inhabitants. This type of suburb has also given rise to much of the speculation regarding the development within the suburb of a new way of life. Whyte is one writer who sees the suburb not just as a 'great conglomeration of mass housing but as producing a particular way of life'. Whyte, although writing about American

TABLE 3

Suburban Typology

*Type of Suburb**	*Examples of this type†*
1. Middle-class planned residential	Park Forest (USA)[14] Levittown (USA)[15] Crestwood Heights (USA)[16] Woodford (UK)[17]
2. Working-class planned residential	Militipas (USA)[18] Greenleigh (UK)[19] Wigston Magna (UK)[20] Becontree (UK)[21]
3. Middle-class unplanned residential	Old Harbour (USA)[22] Hertfordshire commuter village (UK)[23] Nottinghamshire commuter village (UK)[24] Berkshire commuter village (UK)[25] Westchester & Fairfield County (USA)[26]
4. Working-class planned industrial	Liverpool estate (UK)[27] Saltaire (UK)[28] Bournville (UK)[28] Port Sunlight (UK)[28]
5. Working-class unplanned residential	No studies
6. Middle-class planned industrial	No studies
7. Middle-class unplanned industrial	No studies
8. Working-class unplanned industrial	West Ham (UK)[29] Camberwell (UK)[30] Paddington (UK)[29]

* Industrial/residential suburbs are defined by the proportion of people living and working in the area. When this is greater than those commuting to other areas it is an industrial suburb; when more commute than work internally, residential. These criteria are incorporated into the job and commuting ratios discussed in Chapter 3.

† For list of sources see notes 14–30 in chapter notes.

suburbs, could equally well be writing about suburbs elsewhere as well when he writes:

> They [the middle-class, planned, residential suburbs] are a new social institution, and while the variations in them are many, wherever one goes, the courts of Park Forest, the patios of Merced in San Francisco, Philadelphia's Drexelbrook, the new Levittown, Pennsylvania – [there] is unmistakable similarity in the way of life . . . It is a communal way of life.[32]

In the United States this type of suburb is typified by the 'Levittowns' built by a particular builder, J. Levitt & Sons in the Eastern Seaboard States. There are three Levittowns in Long Island (Nassau County), Bucks County (Pennsylvania), and Trenton (New Jersey). The first of these was begun immediately after the Second World War to meet the needs of the returning servicemen. The first Levittown began as the relatively modest venture of providing about 2,000 houses for rental to young ex-servicemen. This number, due to the demand for housing in America at this time, was increased to 4,000 at the end of 1947 and to 6,000 in 1948. After 1948 as a result of the Federal Housing Act of that year, the remainder of the houses in Levittown were built for sale rather than rental. The suburb was completed in 1951, by which time there were houses for 15,000 families. The first Levittown was planned at each stage rather than having an overall plan, which meant that facilities such as schools, playgrounds and a community centre were added later, not being part of the original plan. In the late Levittowns, however, these facilities were incorporated into the overall plan and built at the same time as the houses. The houses were built in all the Levittowns to a standard pattern, and in the first were either known as 'Cape Cods' or after 1949 'Ranch houses'. These two types were both basically ones with four downstairs rooms and an expansion attic which had room for the creation of a further two rooms. The ranch house was built to the same pattern only slightly larger. The builder attempted to provide some variety in the otherwise standardized design by using different colours and different façades, and setting the houses at different distances from the roads which were planned in gentle curves rather than in straight lines. One innovation of the Levittowns which has come to typify the suburb was the sixteen-foot picture windows of the living rooms, which according to the critics merely framed another picture window in one of the other houses of the suburb. The principal features hence of the Levittowns are the standard design and plan of the suburb which produces a high degree of homogeneity in its populations, attracting people with similar occupations and income levels. These people for the most part were, and still are, the rising middle class of American society.

The second type of suburb is that of the working-class, planned, residential suburb. The physical and dominant activity aspects are not markedly dissimilar to the first type, except in Britain, whereas most middle-class suburbs have been the product of private developers most working-class suburbs have been the product of local authority re-housing and overspill schemes. This means that for many of the residents the move to the suburbs was not a planned one voluntarily entered into but was the result of local authority decisions. The study which highlights the characteristics of this type of suburb most clearly is the study by Willmott of the London County Council housing estate at Becontree in Essex. Building of this suburb began in 1921 and was completed in 1934 by which time there were 27,000 houses and a population of 90,000, making the area the biggest housing estate in the world at that time, and also the largest planned residential working-class suburb. When the suburb was completed there was little industry in the area, Fords only coming to Dagenham, near by, in 1931, so most of the workers returned to London each day to work. In 1931 the proportion of daily commuters was two thirds of the working population. By 1958 the proportion of commuters to London had declined to just under one third and over half of the population worked in either Dagenham, Ilford or Barking which are the neighbouring local authority areas. Throughout its development the estate has been an entirely residential area and this has led to its having a 'general atmosphere of a vast flatness, openness and uniformity'.[33] Willmott examines work, family life, the extent to which kinship is important, friends and neighbour relations and compares his findings with the old working-class area of Bethnal Green on the one hand and Woodford (middle-class suburb) on the other, and concludes that the estate is closer to the old area of Bethnal Green. Willmott, in assessing the change in Becontree, says that the estate is 'more the physical environment of a strung-out suburb'[34] but the people have not adopted the pattern of the middle-class suburbanite. This lack of middle-class suburban life style is attributed to the working-class nature of the estate of Becontree which serves to 'insulate the people from middle-class influences'. Other studies which bear out these findings are those of Mogey, Jennings and Young and Willmott.[35] These studies of the working-class suburb both in Britain and in the United States of America have not found any evidence to suggest the development of a new way of life.

The third type of suburb is the unplanned residential middle-class suburb. This type is more complex than either of the first two due to a large extent to its pattern of growth. This type of suburb has had a much longer period of development than either of the first two types and is faced with rather different problems, those of the adaptation to the new residents by the host population and vice versa, with not the creation of new institutions but with the modification or even the replacement of existing ones.

This type has been studied in America by Dobriner in a rural village which he calls 'Old Harbour', which is situated on the coast of New England and has been in existence for over 300 years. Old Harbour had been built originally on sea trading and small manufacturing. These activities, however, began to decline towards the end of the nineteenth century. The community received two sets of immigrants which in turn provided extra money and stimulation for the community. The first wave of newcomers came during the nineteenth century from the neighbouring urban areas, some thirty-six miles away. These newcomers were the new industrial aristocracies and they built large houses and owned the various estates which existed in the area around the old village. This group tended to keep themselves apart from the rest of the village, hence no great changes were brought about in the life of Old Harbour. By the 1920s, the urban areas of America were undergoing a period of rapid expansion and these resulted in the urban population spreading out into the surrounding rural communities. This rapid growth of the cities' hinterlands was the cause of the second set of newcomers to Old Harbour. During the 1920s the first commuters were found travelling to the city from the Old Harbour area. The final explosion of the urban population into the countryside and into Old Harbour came in the period immediately after the Second World War, the period 1945–55 seeing a doubling of the population of the old village of Old Harbour and the creation of two distinct communities, the old village, surrounded by the new estates of the suburbanites. Dobriner, describing the kind of suburban development which has taken place, writes:

Out along the periphery of the old village, up on what were farmlands five years ago, out along the land necks reaching towards the bay, down in the cave valleys and up among the woody ridges, range the dwellings of suburbia. Here among the asbestos shingle or 'hand split shabes' the plastic and the stainless steel, the picture window, the two-car garage and pint sized dining areas, the weathered wagon wheels and . . . strawberry barrel, live the suburbanites in their multi-level reconstruction of Colonial America . . . This is no proletarian Levittown. 'Peppermill Village' starts with a 'minimum' house of just seven rooms and two baths for $22,500 and goes on up . . . antiquity early American, 'good taste'. The limited Dream finds a concretized expression of the poet's myth in 'Authentic Farmhouse Reconstructions' and the 'Modernized New England Village'.[36]

The suburbanites moving into Old Harbour were then high-income executives and professionals (upper middle class); as individuals they were occupationally upwardly mobile. Their jobs gave them a greater prestige than that of the original inhabitants and their primary orientation was not to the local community of Old Harbour but to the metropolis. This image of the new suburbanite is contrasted with the original inhabitants of Old Harbour who are seen as localistic, Protestant and economically comfortable, conservative and middle-class. The majority of the villagers are merchants and small manufacturers, and are described as 'nineteenth-century entrepreneurs' at one point by Dobriner. For these people Old Harbour is their community, it is an end in itself rather than merely a means to an end which is located in the metropolitan world rather than the local community. The structure of such a suburb and its 'problems' obviously differ from those of the planned suburb as here there was an existing population, existing institutions such as schools, churches, local government and shops and these were all involved in questions of how far they were to adapt to accommodate the newcomers. The central source of conflict in Old Harbour centred around the educational system with the newcomers wanting to spend considerably more on education and more anxious to adopt the latest educational ideas and methods than were the original inhabitants of Old Harbour.

Turning from Dobriner's study to that of Pahl,[37] who studied a number of communities in Hertfordshire UK, a similar picture of the *reluctant suburb* can be seen. The migration of new population into the communities studied were predominantly although not exclusively middle-class. It began in the 1920s as in the previous case and again underwent a rapid increase in the post-war periods. In the three villages studied, 66 per cent, approximately 50 per cent and 43 per cent of the migrants had arrived since 1945. The middle-class nature of the migrant population is shown by the analysis of the proportion in each class who were 'established' and 'newcomers'. For the middle class (defined on the basis of the Registrar-General's occupational categories) the proportions were 19 per cent established (pre-1945) to 81 per cent newcomers. For the working class the figures were 71 per cent established and 29 per cent newcomers. The developments within the three villages varied a little with the most exclusive and expensive being in Tewin Wood. This area in the early 1960s when studied was being developed by a North London builder with 'a choice of standard, split-level and continental designs in woodland setting – 3, 4 and 5 bedrooms, ½ acre plots, central heating optional; £6,500–£9,000'.[38] This kind of development is reminiscent of Old Harbour. The entry of the new middle-class elements led to both social and residential segregation between the different groups in the population. Again the suburb that had been created was not one of design but a creation of two separate 'communities' one oriented to the locality (the established, predominantly working-class villagers) and the other oriented to the metropolis (the newcomer, predominantly middle-class).

The third example is the study of the growth of a reluctant suburb in the area to the south of the city of Nottingham

(UK).[39] Here once again the same kinds of processes were at work: the small-scale movements of population until the post-war period when the pace of migration increased rapidly so that some of the communities doubled between the 1951–61 censuses. This migration from the city was once more predominantly middle-class and its advent led to the creation of separate groups of newcomers and established. These two groups exhibited orientations to the metropolis on the one hand and the local community on the other. The two groups formed by the migration were ones with a differing view as to the functions and value of the local community and hence conflicts arose as to the importance, value and organization of particular community institutions and practices.

The three suburban types examined so far have all been purely residential. Also on the peripheries of the cities there have grown up new areas which have an industrial base. These suburbs are created to aid the city in its decentralization and congestion problems created not just by overcrowding but by the commuting of the suburban populations by train, bus and car. The industrial suburbs which have grown up of this type have been largely working-class as the housing has been developed in association with the industrial development. Within the housing estates of the industrial suburb the layout and general planning is similar to any other planned suburb; the special feature is the relationship of the workers to specific industries sited within the area. Hence there is little commuting from such suburbs to other areas within the city. An example of a planned working-class industrial suburb is the one discussed by Mitchell and Lupton.[40] This suburb of Liverpool grew up to provide housing for workers engaged in aircraft production during wartime. Other examples are cited by Harris in his work based on the American census of 1941 and the writings on the development of the suburbs of Paris.[41] Where the working-class industrial suburb is planned it corresponds in all respects to type two except for the provision of employment within the suburb which creates perhaps a greater underlying unity to the suburb than is possible where this is absent. The suburbs created by nineteenth-century philanthropists at Saltaire (1851), Bournville (1879) and Port Sunlight (1888) are also most appropriately seen as suburbs of this type as they were provided by the founders to house their own workers in better conditions than existed at that time in the congested city centres.

The four remaining types are all possible types but they are not ones which have as yet become very important. There are working-class elements usually of the higher grades within the manual population who move into unplanned suburbs. But as it is clearly shown by Pahl[42] these are a minority, hence the character of the suburb is not determined by the working-class migrants; rather they are more likely to be the members of this class who are upwardly mobile to a middle-class style of living which is associated in their minds with a suburban style. Also because moving to the suburb which is not created by a local authority means buying a house, this kind of suburb is limited to the more affluent sections of the community. For these various reasons there are few if any suburbs which could accurately be described as unplanned working-class suburbs. Neither are there likely to be many middle-class industrial suburbs because of the non-manual nature of middle-class employment. The last type of suburb distinguished is that of the working-class industrial suburb which is unplanned. These are the suburbs, like West Ham in London, which grew up during the nineteenth century as a mixture of industrial and residential developments with their growth being essentially a piecemeal and haphazard process. This same kind of process of industrial and housing growth is also visible around other major metropolises; this is demonstrated, for example, in studies of the growth of the suburbs of Paris. This would also appear to be the category in which to place those suburbs which originally began as unplanned middle-class areas but have subsequently been vacated and turned into working-class suburbs of mixed residential, commercial and industrial use. This process can be quite clearly seen in the development of London's suburbs in the nineteenth and twentieth centuries, for example, Camberwell and Paddington.

So far it has not been considered whether or not the new town constitutes a type of suburb. The degree to which the new towns have a separate industrial and commercial structure and are therefore consequently not dependent upon a city for its services would be the best basis upon which the question could be resolved. If the new town is considered to be a suburb, then it is obviously a planned one. The study of Levittown by Gans is in effect the study of a new town created by the builder completely independently of any existing community. Gans clearly considers Levittown a suburb as it is not independent but in fact highly dependent upon the city for the work of its inhabitants and the provision of a wide range of services. The case, however, of Britain's new towns is not as clear-cut as this, and they could in fact reflect a substantially different picture. The new towns were envisaged as separate and independent entities to act as a counter-attraction to the pull of major cities, in particular London. Hence they were planned as total communities having both residential accommodation (virtually all there was in Levittown) and an industrial and commercial structure to provide employment for as many as possible of the inhabitants within the new town. The success of the new towns in achieving independence has, however, been variable. In a recent study of the eight new towns in the London area,[43] the degree of independence is assessed by means of an 'independence index' which is a measure of the extent to which a town is self-contained with regard to journey to work. From the examination of the eight towns on the index it was found that six increased their degree of independence in the period from 1951–66 and in Basildon and Stevenage the index more than doubled over the period. On the basis of this evidence there would not be a great deal of justification for terming the new town a suburb. The relationship between social class structure and the structure of the new towns is also far from simple as has recently been pointed out in a study of Crawley.[44] This study shows that there has been a steady movement towards residential segregation based upon social class within the new towns even though they began as ostensibly integrated communities without the residential segregation by class which is a characteristic of all other urban areas in Britain. On the whole, therefore, it does not seem to be reasonable to consider the new town to be a suburban area as it lacks the basic condition of the suburb, that of dependence upon the city, the dependence showing itself in high levels of commuting. The suburb also has a high level of homogeneity of population (in terms of class or stage in the family cycle) which, partly because of its size, the new town does not possess. The new town is at least in theory a complete community whereas the suburb is only a partial community.

6 The Suburbs and Work Ethics

In the past it has been assumed that because work took up the greater part of his time, it must provide a central life interest for the individual. This view has been increasingly challenged as studies have pointed to a variety of attitudes towards work within industrial societies. There would appear to be currently three main views of work. These are the Protestant ethic, the social ethic and the domestic ethic. Each of those three would appear to be present within certain occupational and residential groups, the last two in particular having a close association with writings on the suburb.

The 'traditional' view of work, which some still hold to be the dominant one in our society, is the one which has arisen from the Protestant ethic. According to some writers, particularly Max Weber,[1] this ethic provided the moral and religious justification for the present industrial capitalist system which predominates in Western societies. The essential consequence of this ethic was to give a central place within the individual's life to his work and to make the work sphere the one in which his success was measured and from which he derived his personal satisfactions. This ethic was held most strongly among the professional and entrepreneurial classes, the latter forming the backbone of the new industrial system which emerged with the Industrial Revolution. The professional groups held strongly to the idea that work involved a 'calling' or moral obligation to perform it to the best of one's ability and this concept is still found in the strongly held 'service to others' ethic of many professions, e.g. medicine and the Church. Outside of these groups it is difficult to determine the extent of the ethic's influence over the entire population. In so far as these groups were those which set the tone and conditioned the values of society the ethic had influence over the entire population and formed the desired attitude to work of all those who wished to achieve social and occupational mobility. However, apart from the socially mobile members of the working class who adopted these values as part of their mobility, and certain 'craft' workers, there is little evidence of the ethic's influence upon the manual workers as a whole. For the manual workers work was, and still largely is, an activity done for the end product, the wage, rather than in order to derive some kind of intrinsic satisfaction in the performance of the 'work' itself. The growth of alternative ethics to the Protestant ethic have been the result of two separate changes. The first is a change in the industrial, occupational order which has led to the creation of a greater variety of non-manual employment. The old-style entrepreneur was seen as the owner, director and manager of the factory who was in charge of both day to day activities and long-term policy making. With the growth in size of enterprise, particularly after the advent of the joint stock company these three functions became separate and shareholders, boards of directors, and numerous managerial positions were created. With the creation of this managerial structure there was an increase in the number of routine clerical and lower-grade managerial staff. In addition to these changes within explicitly industrial organizations has been the growth of various government administrations again creating an increasingly differentiated non-manual population. Not only has the category of entrepreneur changed but also that of the professions, with the growth of the so-called new professions, for example, scientists, technologists, social workers. How far do these groups share the 'traditional' professional view of work as a calling? All these various changes have created new categories of workers who do not necessarily ascribe to the traditional ethics of the non-manual group. As these are new groups do they also have a new ethic or do they hold some modified version of an existing ethic?

The second change which has also had an effect upon the ethics people hold in regard to work is the growth of the suburb. As illustrated earlier, the suburb changed during the nineteenth century from the retreat of the well-to-do to the home of more and more groups in the population. This movement of families from the older centres of the cities to a new house in a new area presented the family with new problems and new opportunities to change their pattern of living. The research of some investigators suggests that this migration has had an influence at least as definite as the changes in the occupational structure upon the attitudes to work formulated by the individual, particularly among the 'new' occupational groups within the non-manual hierarchy (the salaried employees, the managers, salesmen, scientists and technologists).

The alternative ethics which have been put forward are the 'social ethic' and the 'domestic ethic'. In contrast to the Protestant ethic the social ethic lays great stress upon being well adjusted to social and organizational life both within the work and in the new work spheres. The emphasis upon group life and adjustment has its origins in both the human relations school of industrial sociology with its insistence upon the creation of groups within the work sphere to create happy efficient workers, and the study of suburbs where intensive social group life has been found. The social ethic is defined as 'that contemporary body of thought which makes morally legitimate the pressures of society against the individual. The major propositions are three: a belief in the group as the source of creativity; a belief in 'belongingness' as the ultimate need of the individual, and a belief in the application of science to achieve this "belongingness".'[2]

The typical picture drawn by those who support this ethic is of individuals who are committed, not to their work as such, but to the organization in which they work, which tends to intrude upon all aspects of their lives. This commitment to the organization results in the belief that success will come through conformity to the organization, through being a good joiner and mixer rather than being original or outstanding at one's actual work. This same belief in conformity is also the dominant theme of social life, of the residential community, mostly the suburbs, where these individuals live. In these communities the individual is judged by his willingness to be sociable and to join in the formal and informal system of group relations which produces the new communal way of life. This way of life is thus the consequence rather than the cause of the adoption by its residents of the new social ethic. Therefore, the suburb is not given here a particularly positive role in bringing about changes in the individual's attitudes towards work, rather it is seen as the place where changes produced in the work sphere are made manifest in social activity.

The alternative to this social ethic sees a rather different reaction by individuals to the change in his occupational world and his living. Because of the increasingly specialized nature of work life in modern organizations the individual now finds that promotion within his work is more difficult. The tendency to recruit people from outside and assigning of particular qualifications to each grade has made difficult if not impossible an individual's ability to be occupationally successful beyond certain clearly defined limits. This has led to the workers, particularly in the lower sections of the non-manual hierarchy, turning their attention away from work towards other spheres in which to seek their satisfaction and fulfilment and adopting a purely instrumental attitude to work. This new attitude finds expression in the work sphere by the increasing number of white-collar workers who are members of militant trade unions, engaged in raising their income levels. It is the reaction of the individual out of the work sphere which leads to the rise of the domestic ethic. This is the result in part of the reduction of opportunity in the work sphere and in part due to the positive role of the suburb. The suburbs to which people have been moving offer them the opportunity to find satisfaction in family and house-centred activities. The domestic ethic is hence characterized by such goods as 'suburban peace and domesticity' and is shown in the tremendous growth of what has been termed by some writers as the 'work of suburbia', the do-it-yourself home improvements and the strong emphasis upon family, home-bound leisure activities rather than work or community-based activities.

To evaluate these three 'ethics' and to estimate the influence of the suburb upon their formation it is necessary to look at the various studies which have examined the various groups of workers in both their occupational and residential setting. The three groups of workers that are distinguishable are the manual

Typical middle class low density suburb laid out in gentle curving roads and cul-de-sacs. Note also presence of gardens and trees giving the whole a very different look to the stark bareness of the working class suburb.

Typical of working class suburbs of a planned type with its virtually identical houses, laid out in straight lines with the occasional cul-de-sac. The wide straight roads and lack of trees together with the sameness of the houses gives the area a bare, uniform appearance.

Reluctant suburb. This shows how the village grows through the addition of new small housing developments around the edge creating a low density unplanned suburb. The houses here are of many types built at different periods, mostly since 1945.

Middle class suburb showing the overall layout of curving roads and cul-de-sacs, popular with private developers in the inter-war and immediate post-war periods.

Wedge shaped suburban development at Okadama on the outskirts of Sapporo, Japan. Note the higher densities and more geometric layout than that shown in the previous examples of British suburbs.

Development of suburban flats, showing one of the longest flats in Europe, on the edge of Rouen. The development here being clearly influenced by Le Corbusier's conception of the city of towers within a park.

Another example of flat development in French suburban areas.

The complex illustrated here provides more variety in design and although French is not unlike suburban development found around cities in Britain.

workers, the older professional and entrepreneurial group and the newer non-manual groups.

The first group of manual workers has been studied on both sides of the Atlantic to try to determine the influence of modern industrial organization upon their view of work. From this research the studies of Dubin,[3] Weiss and Kahn,[4] Friedman and Havighurst,[5] Chinoy[6] and Berger,[7] are relevant to our understanding of the attitudes of the American worker, and the work of Goldthorpe, Lockwood,[8] Zweig[9] and Young and Willmott,[10] for the British worker.

The work of Dubin was concerned with examining the assumption that work was a central life interest for the industrial worker and investigated 491 employees of three mid-western plants living in communities ranging from 35,000 to 125,000. Dubin found that for only 24 per cent of his sample was work a central life interest. For the majority work was a means to an end, a way of acquiring income rather than an end in itself hence their involvement was purely instrumental. Dubin commenting on his finding writes: 'The factory and factory work as sources of personal satisfaction, pride, satisfying human associations, perhaps even of pleasure in expressing what Veblen called "instinct of workmanship", seem clearly subordinated in the American Scene.'[11]

Further Dubin found that for only 10 per cent was work the place where individuals established their most important social relationships. The absence of work as a central life interest did not necessarily lead the workers to a higher level of organizational involvement in their leisure-time activities, rather their leisure time appears to have been spent with their families and in informal group activities. In another study by Weiss and Kahn, which was not concerned purely with manual workers, an attempt was made to discover the way in which work was defined by different occupational groups. This study was based on a probability sample of 371 men aged 21 and over, living in Detroit. For the four groups of manual workers distinguished, work as a necessary though not enjoyed activity was given most often, except in the unskilled labourers group. However, among the labourers and factory workers working within large-scale organizations the definition of work as a scheduled activity was given by 35 per cent of the factory workers and 47 per cent of the labourers. This definition indicates the extent to which the workers felt their job allowed them no room for personal activity, that all their work was within clearly defined limits. From this study what is quite clear is that none of the manual groups saw their work in other than instrumental terms, not even the craft workers who have been considered by some to be a group in which the Protestant ethic has had some influence. Hence the picture of Dubin's workers is reinforced. A further study by Friedman and Havighurst also distinguished between a number of groups of manual workers in order to discover whether or not the workers in different industrial settings held different attitudes towards their work. The groups were steelworkers and coal-miners as representative of traditional heavy industries, and craftsmen. Of these three groups again the last one would be where, if anywhere, the Protestant ethic would be held. It was found that the workers in the mines and steelworks saw work on the whole as having no other meaning than that of earning money. For the skilled craftsmen, however, there were 25 per cent who saw their work as a purposeful activity through which they were able to express themselves. This compared with only 10 per cent who saw work simply as a source of money. This research gives some support to the view that skilled craftsmen, who are in fact a declining feature in the modern industrial society, do have more resemblance to the work ethic of higher socio-economic groups than have the rest of the manual working class. The findings here were based on a sample of 450 skilled craftsmen and 281 steelworkers and miners. The last study of workers in their occupational setting can be linked with a study of workers in their residential setting. These are the studies of Chinoy and Berger. Chinoy was concerned to explore the relationship between the automobile workers and the American Dream of individual success through achievement in the work sphere. His findings were based on sixty-two workers over the age of 30 whom he interviewed. This evidence he supplemented with statistical data from the plant, working for a time in the plant and talking with management and trade union officials. The kind of question he was concerned about was what influence upon the worker's commitment to the American Dream of success was the 'nice little modern house' and also the question of the extent to which the 'domestic package was expandable'. The success ideology of America meant that workers should work for, and be anxious to achieve promotion through, the firm. However, the various levels of the firm were filled from outside, which frustrated the worker's desires. Also the ideology stressed individual action and achievement yet the factory demanded increasingly collective action. Chinoy hence found that most of the men did not have a very strong commitment to their work. Their strongest commitment was to goals outside work. If they still desired success through work this was expressed in the desire to start a business of their own. The men who had the clearest defined out-of-work goals were those married and in their late twenties and early thirties who had not acquired any seniority. Berger who studied the working-class suburb of Militipas claimed that his study could be seen as the twin of Chinoy's who centres his study on the factory whereas Berger centres his on the suburb. For his suburban population Berger is quite sure that work and achievement are solely a matter of money. The working class of Berger's suburb have, through their income, been able to raise their standard of living; they have been able to buy houses in the suburbs and therefore have been able to turn their attention to the delights of home making in a way that had never been open to them before.

From this brief look at some of the research on the American working class and the role of the suburb, it is possible to see that only small groups of skilled craft workers hold anything other than an instrumental view of work. However, because interest in the working-class suburb in America is relatively new there is only Berger's study which concerns itself with an explicitly working-class suburban population. The evidence here, together with that of Chinoy and Dubin, supports the view that the suburb is the arena in which the 'domestic ethic' is allowed to flourish.

Moving from American studies to British working-class studies those of Goldthorpe and Lockwood and Zweig are of particular value. Goldthorpe and Lockwood studied affluent workers employed in three progressive industries in Luton in the early 1960s. They found that in all cases the workers expressed an instrumental attitude towards their work. Many of the workers had moved to work in these Luton firms from other parts of the country for the higher wages offered. The workers expressing this attitude lived in some cases in their own houses in new 'suburban areas' of the town. The features of the job that kept them in their present employment were those of pay and security. For none of them was it the intrinsic value attached to the job itself. The British writers, like Dubin and other American writers, found that this lack of seeing their jobs as a central life interest did not lead to an increase in their organizational involvement. The average number of organizations to which they belonged was 1·5, (which included principally working-class organizations such as trade unions and working men's clubs) and for their wives the number of organizations was 0·5. Zweig, from his studies of the British worker, comes to a similar conclusion that work for manual workers is an instrumental activity. Zweig, summarizing his position, writes: 'Most men believe that the function of a job, even an interesting job is primarily to provide money for the comforts, amenities and pleasures of life.'[12] Evidence which relates to the suburban influence upon these attitudes towards work can be drawn from the research of the Institute of Community Studies into working-class population in East London. In their study of *Family and Kinship in East London*, Young and Wilmott examine the influence of moving East-Enders from Bethnal Green, a 'traditional' working-class area to a new housing area at Greenleigh. In the East End the people lived in houses owned by others and hence the families were reluctant to spend much time and money upon the appearance of the house. The property was also old and in many cases dilapidated. However, at Greenleigh the family moved into a brand new house which provided a stimulus for them to become more home conscious and this brought about the house-centred spirit. The home and family of marriage became for the Greenleigh dwellers the focus of their lives far more than they ever were in the East End. The lives of these new 'suburban' dwellers became centred on the house whereas in the East End they were focused upon other people outside the house, often members of their extended kinship network. The workers here have not changed their attitude to work so much as their attitude towards and the importance they attach to their house, and this is a change of attitude initiated by the suburb. This change is also at the very heart of the idea of the 'domestic ethic'. The study of P. Willmott[13] of the Becontree housing estate which also was established to re-house London's working class supports the general conclusions of the study of Greenleigh, with the one exception that the status element in the competition between the individual domestic units is less strong in Becontree due to its greater insulation from middle-class groups.

From the research studies of the British manual worker examined here support is again found for the rejection of any kind of non-instrumental view of work within the working class. Moreover, there is some quite strong evidence that when working-class people move into new areas which are adjacent to middle-class suburban areas there is the development of the third ethic distinguished, the 'domestic ethic'.

The second major group which has to be examined is that with which the Protestant ethic has always been associated, the professional and higher executive, managerial groups in society. Evidence can again be drawn from a number of surveys which explored the work attitudes of these groups. The study by Friedman and Havighurst, referred to above, also considered the meaning attached to work by physicians. They found that the greatest number of responses favoured the view that work was a service to others, which indicates that at least a third held the traditional professional view regarding work. The other meanings which were given prominence were work as an activity through which the individual obtained the prestige and respect of others, and work as a purposeful activity. The physicians in the sample did not see any sharp divisions between their work and their non-work activities as do manual workers. This study although a valuable indicator of the meaning attached by physicians was based on a very small sample (39), hence has to be treated with caution. The study of Weiss and Kahn also separated out professionals and managers and proprietors. For the professional group (29) they found a majority 55 per cent defined work as an activity which was necessary though not enjoyed, which does not suggest a great deal of enthusiasm for work as a central life interest. Only 7 per cent gave work as a socially useful activity, which is perhaps the category which would include those who held a non-instrumental definition of work. For the managers and proprietors the same category of necessary though not enjoyed received the most support (44 per cent), and was followed by scheduled or paid activity (26 per cent), presumably indicating that a proportion of this category were in middle managerial positions within organizations where they were mainly carrying out the orders of others rather than indicating policy. However, again the evidence was drawn from small samples (29 and 27 respectively). This could account for the high professional instrumental response and the conflict between the research and that of Havighurst and Friedman. A study by Morse and Weiss[14] which is also concerned with this group and the nature of their involvement in work drew a distinction between the professionals who stressed the content of the job and saw their work as something which incorporated a sense of accomplishment, and managers who saw their source of satisfaction much more simply in the level of their salaries. A study which brings together both the occupational context and the suburban is that of Crestwood Heights, which is a study of a Canadian suburb of Toronto. The residents of Crestwood Heights were mostly members of the upper middle class, of professional and business executives who had achieved a fair degree of success in their occupational spheres and were therefore wealthy enough to afford to buy a house in Crestwood Heights. For these Crestwood Heights men personal satisfaction and achievement were to be measured by the height the individual had reached in his occupational hierarchy but the emphasis was on individual achievement rather than organizational involvement. There appears, however, to be some doubt in the minds of the investigators about whether or not the activity which leads to success has to be one which brings an intrinsic reward; rather for many the activity seems to be a means to an end, which is the achievement of material rewards. Seeley *et al.* wrote: 'The basis of their career is not an entirely purposeful course . . . criterion is that he had to be successful, which is different from the concept of work as a calling or moral obligation . . . priority in planning a career given to material rewards.'[15] This does represent clearly a move away from the traditional Protestant ethic. This shift is further emphasized when they write while discussing the family: 'Cash income is all important to the solidarity of the Crestwood Heights family since upon it depends the social status of the family which determines the sense of belonging to the community.'[16]

In Crestwood Heights the picture which emerges is far from clear; on the one hand the career is of central importance, on the other it is the cash income from the career rather than the career itself that is more important. There is evidence, therefore, of at least a degree of instrumentality and a shift from the traditional Protestant ethic within groups which have always been assumed to be the ones in which it is most clearly expressed. The writers of Crestwood Heights also fail to make clear the factors which produce the change in work attitude. Is it because these individuals have all achieved their occupational ambitions and hence are developing alternative goals, or is there some kind of influence exerted by the suburb of Crestwood Heights which is producing a new kind of social or domestic ethic?

The evidence of the work attitudes of these two groups within Britain and in particular the relationship of the suburb is not very extensive. Studies by educational sociologists of the teaching profession have shown that for many this is becoming increasingly one in which the financial rewards are of prime importance both as an attraction to the job and as a source of dissatisfaction within the profession. Apart from this little is known with any great accuracy of the prevailing work ethics of the traditional professions and the higher grades of the managerial and entrepreneurial groups. Studies of these groups in suburban contexts are equally lacking. Some evidence, although limited, is available from the author's own study of two middle-class unplanned, residential suburbs situated adjacent to the cities of Bristol and Nottingham. In this study a similar kind of analysis of work definition to that of Weiss and Kahn was attempted. However, the results were very different, indicating certain cultural differences between the two countries, with the single most important definition of work (in the British sample) being as a productive activity, rather than as a necessary though not enjoyed activity. Using categories similar to Weiss and Kahn, 51 per cent of the professional group in the sample (54) gave work as a productive activity, this compares with 70 per cent of the managerial group. When rather more elaborate categories were used one third of the professional group gave work as a paid activity, and 20 per cent as an enjoyable and satisfying activity. For the managerial group the second most important conception of work after paid activity, was as a routine activity. Overall the definitions offered by both groups, apart from 25 per cent of the professionals, suggest an instrumental attitude to work.

From the evidence discussed here from both the United States and Britain there is little doubt that there are groups of professionals which still hold to the traditional view of work expressed in the Protestant ethic. However, there is also evidence that there are groups who hold alternative views regarding work which show at least a greater degree of instrumentality than has been the case in the commonly held view of the work ethics of professional and higher managerial groups. It is not possible, however, due to the lack of evidence, to say whether or not the degree of instrumentality is related to the suburb.

The third group which was distinguished are by far the most interesting in regard to the general question of the role of the suburb, because much of the argument for the rival ethics has been based upon studies of such new non-manual occupational groups. Some of the studies which have already been considered also have evidence which helps in the clarification of the attitudes of this particular group. The study by Friedman and Havighurst examined, in addition to those of manual workers and physicians, the attitudes of sales personnel. For the seventy-four sales persons in the study work was seen as a purposeful activity by 26 per cent and a source of contacts and associates by a further 20 per cent and routine by 21 per cent. This pattern of response presents if anything a picture of a group without a clearly defined work ethic, some seeing it in 'traditional middle-class' terms whereas others are expressing the instrumental view of the working class. Weiss and Kahn also distinguish sales and clerical groups, in addition to professional and managerial, within their non-manual group. For the sales personnel they find 80 per cent consider work to be a necessary though not enjoyed activity, which clearly indicates a marked degree of instrumentality. For clerical workers the two main definitions were work as necessary though not enjoyed (45 per cent) and work as a scheduled activity (20 per cent). However, the size of these two groups in this study were only twenty respondents in each category, hence these results can serve only as an indication of the likely attitudes. A study which deals explicitly with a quasi-professional group which falls into this category is that of Orzack[17] who studied the extent to which 150 male nurses employed in public and private hospitals and a state mental hospital in a mid-west city considered their work to be a central life interest. The survey used the central life interest scale devised by Dubin for his study of industrial workers. Orzack found that for four out of five of the nurses work and workplace were central life interests. This greater commitment to work was reflected in the tendency of the workers to have their friends and informal groups based on their work. The 21 per cent who did not give work as a central life interest were seen to be those who had little dedication to their professional career because of other influences and responsibilities, like their families and homes. Hence, for this group in contrast to the sales workers and clerical workers examined, work did still play the major role in their lives and their work ethics have greatest resemblance to that of the 'traditional Protestant ethic' of the established professional groups. However, this finding may well be peculiar to nursing where there is still a strong influence of service ethics which have been prominent in medicine and hence more resistant to wider societal changes. Other studies of newer professional groups of scientists and technologists by, for example, Cotgrove[18] and Prandy[19] in Britain do not bear out Orzack's conclusions. Cotgrove's study is based upon interviews with ninety-four technicians and was part of an exploratory study, hence its findings are only tentative. The majority of the technicians saw their work as a means of obtaining non-work satisfactions. Of the five features of work given as of most importance, pay was given most often (90 per cent) followed by security (75 per cent) and interesting work (72 per cent). Pay was also mentioned most frequently as a source of dissatisfaction. When the question of work expectations and satisfactions were examined in relation to family centredness it was found that those stressing the extrinsic element of their work, e.g. pay, were much more family centred than those expressing intrinsic satisfactions (83 per cent compared to 42 per cent). One final point of relevance from this study is that the technicians not only saw their own work as a means to an end but also the work of others in similar situations. For evidence of the attitude to work held by the clerical workers within industrial organizations and low and middle level managements the study by Lockwood and Goldthorpe provides some information. The Luton study as well as sampling the manual worker in the three plants also studied a sample of white-collar workers (54) drawn from only two of the factories. However, these groups showed a much less instrumental view of work than the manual workers, giving greater prominence to work as an activity which was satisfying and enjoyable and showing less explicit concern with the wage level. However, this sample is small and spans a considerable range of levels within the non-manual hierarchy. From these various studies which have focused principally on the occupational setting of the newer professional and middle managerial and white-collar groups there is little evidence to support the Protestant ethic, further they all, with the exception of the nurses, show a considerable degree of instrumentality in their view of work; for most it is a source of pay.

In the studies which have focused more upon the residential rather than the occupational position of these groups, there is found to be a sharp divergence between those who see a new social ethic and those who see a domestic ethic arising. Whyte,[20] in his study of Park Forest, has been at the forefront of the argument in favour of a social ethic. He bases his view on the evidence of Park Forest, a suburb of Chicago, where the population was made up predominantly of young business executives who were busy competing within their respective organizations in building up their positions This meant that they had to be willing to move where their organizations wanted to send them in order to gain promotion. The population hence had an annual turnover of about one third. The residents were employed in many different industries; what united them was that they were all concerned to win approval from their superiors within their organizations and to do this they were anxious to demonstrate their flexibility and ability to adjust. This resulted in the whole life of the community becoming dominated by the ideas of 'adjustment', of 'togetherness', of community-centred activity which would provide both a training ground for the residents in this art and also a kind of stability to help them cope with the problems of geographical mobility. The social life of Park Forest is one which has developed in response to certain demands of the occupations held by the individuals and hence it would only be duplicated where there were similar groups of rising young executives. The weakness of Whyte's whole thesis is simply that Park Forest was not a typical American suburb, it was perhaps not even typical of the middle class, as some others have claimed. What it was and still is typical of is a suburb of a certain type of organization man, who is created by the kinds of industrial organizations of contemporary industrial societies. These men, however, are not the only members of the new middle class, hence as a general alternative ethic the social ethic is clearly not valid.

Another piece of work within America which also tries to relate work and the suburb is that of Riesman[21] who conducted a study of the life, work and values of college seniors in the United States. This study shows that the great majority planned to live in the suburbs and were prepared to sacrifice occupational achievement in favour of the goals of 'suburban peace and domesticity'. The activities which take place within the suburb were for this group the central interests of their lives, rather than work. The 'work of suburbia', Riesman claimed, has replaced the occupational sphere as the central sphere of activities and the one within which personal achievement and success is sought and measured. The work of suburbia consists of do-it-yourself, home improvements, organizational participation of all kinds and most important of all the adoption of a family and child-centred way of life which necessitates the buying of a house and the involvement in the activities of suburbia. Riesman, however, is only talking of projected activities of individuals rather than actual, hence this is less valuable than a study of actual suburbs. Also he makes the assumption which is dubious that to give up occupational achievement as a goal entails sacrifice. What is clear from other evidence is not that people are sacrificing this goal but simply that this never was the goal of the majority.

British studies of suburbs are not very numerous. There is only one study which is explicitly about a middle-class suburb, that of Willmott and Young, apart from the study by the author referred to earlier. In these two middle-class suburbs there was found to be only 54 per cent of the population who saw work as their most important activity, which means that for 46 per cent work had been replaced by other activities. Although 54 per cent saw work as their most important activity, as has already been shown, their conception as to why this is so varies from those who see it as the source of pay hence the basis upon which non-work life is financed to those who see it as an end in itself, this latter group being in the minority. In order to try to assess the relative strengths of the social ethic as against the domestic ethic in these suburbs estimates were attempted of the suburbanites' involvement in community organizational activity rather than domestic and what importance they attached to each. Indicative of the pattern was the finding that for only 3 per cent had membership of voluntary organizations replaced work as a central activity whereas for 50 per cent the desire to improve their house and garden was strongly expressed. The thread running through the evidence collected regarding their work relative to their other activities gave support to the view that rather than work being a central life interest it was the 'domestic' aspect of their situation, the house, family, car etc., which were of central importance.

This same theme is taken up in the study of Woodford by Willmott and Young. The sample is here made up of non-manual workers holding for the most part middle-grade non-manual jobs. There are some people in the suburb who are strongly work centred and who spend long hours at work and virtually the whole of their lives wrapped up in it. These are, however, the exception in Woodford. The majority of the men see work as a five-day-a-week activity and the full two days are spent with their wives and families at the weekend. It is rarely the house and family which takes second place in Woodford; if anything does, it is work, particularly where this is of a rather tedious or monotonous nature which is possibly the case for many of Woodford's lower-paid white-collar workers. The important feature of the suburb which brings about this situation is the fact that the majority of the suburban dwellers (64 per cent) are owner-occupiers. This means that the house provides an endless opportunity for work, for the demonstration of the individual's ability at a whole range of tasks from interior decorating to house alteration to the building of furniture and the laying out of gardens. Each step or scheme for the house is something to be discussed and decided upon by the husband and wife together, although the work was generally done in Woodford by the husband. The tremendous effort and interest in home maintenance was attributed to three reasons: the sheer pride of ownership, the opportunity it gave for demonstrating individual abilities, and the fact that the residents looked upon the house as an investment, buying a house, maintaining and improving it, increased its value and saved money into the bargain. The picture painted here is the epitome of the 'domestic ethic' and it has its origin in the suburb because this is where the opportunity is provided for the outlet of this type of activity. It has been argued that the domestic ethic in such cases as Woodford is the result of failure to succeed in the work sphere, the consequence of blocked promotion chances pushing people out into other spheres to achieve their satisfactions. However, the commitment of Woodford's inhabitants to family or community or both could just as easily be a cause of lack of success in the work sphere and if this were the case then it would be the result of a deliberately taken decision and adoption of a new ethic regarding the way an individual should find success in our society.

The evidence examined makes it quite clear that there is no one ethic with regard to work which is accepted by all occupational groups as 'the ethic'. Hence argument about the role of the suburb in transforming or changing the work ethic of society has to be carefully examined. It is too simple to say, as Whyte does, that the Protestant ethic has been replaced by the social ethic found in the suburbs of America in response to the growth of the large organizations. On the basis of the existing evidence, particularly from British studies, the importance of work in the suburbs is as a provider of income. Suburban people are, on the whole, more interested in their domestic life, in their house, family, garden etc., than they are in their work. This could be due either to occupational or to strictly residential factors. The answer to this cannot be satisfactorily resolved on the basis of present evidence. All that can be said is that the domestic, i.e. suburban ethic, is held most strongly by middle- and lower-grade management and routine white-collar employees and least strongly by professional and higher managerial groups.

7 The Suburb and the Family

The association of the 'domestic ethic' with the suburb has meant that at the heart of much of the writing on the suburban way of life lies the family, in particular the nuclear family. The suburb has had ascribed to it varying degrees of influence upon the present form of the family. The family is crucial both to the decision to move to the suburb and to the whole suburban way of life which has grown up as a substitute or compensation for the reduced influence of family contacts between the nuclear element and its wider kinship universe. The desire for the single-family dwelling house is one of the most powerful influences upon the decision to move to the suburb from the city centre, or to rural areas. This move to the suburb creates a new situation for the family unit as it produces a physical separation from its extended family and promotes greater joint-couple activity and concentration upon the welfare of the children. This change in family structure is also a reflection of the rising social aspirations of the mobile groups and an indicator of their acceptance of the assumed norms of middle-class life.

The prominence of the commitment to the success of the family and a concern for its welfare is to be found in all the studies which have been conducted into why people move to the suburbs. W. Bell[1] for example, distinguishes three basic value differences open to the individual in an industrial society and these he terms familism, consumership and career. Familism is where a high value is placed upon family living, marriage is generally at a relatively young age and is followed by a short childless span and with the arrival of the children the family becomes increasingly child-centred in its activities. Consumership is where possessions and non-work are given the highest priority. The motto of such a group would be 'Have a good time today and let tomorrow care for itself'; the concern with immediate enjoyment rather than with deferred gratification and short-term rather than long-term goals. A career life style is, in contrast, one where the individual spends time and money on his career to the exclusion of all else. The popularity of familism for Bell lies in the desires of Americans since the Second World War to create a better future for their children. The generation taking houses and beginning families in this period had as a recent experience the 1930s period of unemployment and lack of housing in America and the war. The same desire to build a better life for their children is also expressed by people within Britain and was a dominant influence in the planning of new housing areas after the war. In America this desire for the success and future of the children became tied up with the idea of having a single-family dwelling and these were provided in the suburbs. Hence the suburbs took on something of a utopian quality for many individuals, being the arena for a new life to be created, a life which would place high on its list of priorities the family unit and, in particular, the education and development of the children. In order to find out the relative strengths of these three values in the individual's decision to move to the suburbs, Bell studied two Chicago suburbs of Park Ridge and Des Plaines. Of the sample 65 per cent had previously lived in flats in Chicago. 82 per cent of the movers gave essentially family reasons for their decision to move. Further he found that 75 per cent of the lower social status groups and 61 per cent of the higher had familism as their dominant value compared to only 55 per cent of the lower status groups and 45 per cent of the higher status groups in non-suburban Chicago. The suburb is seen by Bell to select differentially those individuals who had familism as their dominant style of life, and the suburb itself only acted as the provider of the house where this value could be most fully expressed. Another American study which also supports the importance of family reasons in the decision to move is that of Munson.[2] This study into people moving into suburbs of Indianapolis found that mothers wanted to live in the suburbs much more often than fathers and that the principal reasons given for preferring a suburban to a city residence were that the former was better for the children as it was cleaner, and the couple moving desired a house with a larger amount of land attached to it. Gans[3] in his study of Levittown (USA) also finds that the reasons for moving are based upon aspirations for single-family houses brought about by the desire to provide better opportunities for family life. The strong association between the desire for improved family living and the suburb is to a large extent due to the fact that these were the only areas where housing was available at the price the majority could afford. Hence there was only a limited degree of final choice being exercised by many of those who moved to the suburbs. This element of choice is greatest for the wealthiest sections of the city population and least for the re-housed working class who are moved to the suburban housing estates. For many of this latter group the move was not in fact initially welcomed because it meant a separation from their wider kinship system and a breakdown of the traditional systems of family support which had provided a whole range of services from obtaining houses and jobs to baby sitting and advice on child rearing. This forced separation of the re-housed families from their kin has led them to adopt a pattern of life very similar to the middle class, of joint role activity of the husband and wife within the home, which gives the appearance of the 'familistic values' but is not in fact the result of a conscious choice of the kind of ethic by the families.

Consequently, it is not correct to attribute all movements to the suburbs to the adoption of or the desire to adopt familistic values. Rather these are in many cases the consequence of a move which was dictated by other reasons. This kind of case, where the values develop after the move, is the one studied by Young and Willmott[4] where they find an increased emphasis upon family relationships of a nuclear type and a decline in the importance of the older kin network as a result of the population being moved from Bethnal Green in the East End of London some twenty-five miles further out to a new housing estate at Greenleigh.

It has been claimed by some writers that the family within the suburb demonstrates a new form which is not found in either rural or urban areas. American writers have been the most extravagant in their claims for a new form of the family; British writers have been happy to suggest that modifications have taken place within the family structure. Mowrer,[5] discussing the suburban family in America, isolates three factors as influential in producing the changed form of the family in the suburb. These are prosperity, the encouragement of home ownership by the Government (through F.H.A. and V.A.) and the suburban vision. The last of these is the most important for the examination of the distinct role of the suburb. The suburban vision is related to the struggle for status in American society and this, Mowrer feels, lies at the heart of the suburb and hence is a crucial influence upon family structure and behaviour. He writes: 'There is no more culturally acceptable symbol of superior status than living in the suburbs.'[6] The suburban dweller is seen as being able to indulge in a home life where he may demonstrate his individual achievement in his pride of ownership and workmanship in his 'cultivation of flowers, manicuring of lawns and shrubs'. These influences upon the style of family living have led to the suggestion that a new form is emerging with the following characteristics. Firstly family unity is increased through a common interest in and concern for the house. Secondly there is greater participation of the family as a unit in local institutions. Thirdly role differentiation within the family is becoming less rigid resulting in greater husband–wife co-operation with the major activities of the family. Not only is there greater co-operation but there is a greater degree of flexibility and interchange of roles. For example, the husband helps with household activities and the children, and the wife helps with the household maintenance and the garden.

In the study of Crestwood Heights by Sim *et al.*,[7] the single-family house was seen to have a central role in the family's activities. They write:

> The house is a valuable means of ensuring privacy in a crowded city, a vehicle for enforcing family solidarity and conformity, a place to practise and perfect consumption skills, a major item of personal property, which, for the head of the family (and to a lesser degree for his wife and children) stands as a concrete symbol of his status and a visible sign of his success.[8]

Here there is evidence then of two of the factors distinguished by Mowrer, the importance of the house and the suburban vision which concerned the central importance of status. The whole of

Crestwood Heights' society at one level is geared to the children who are taught early independence and the importance of individual achievement. The family has become democratic rather than authoritarian in its decision making in that the resolution of conflicts between parents and children is attempted through discussion rather than by the imposition of parental views. The roles of the various members within the family have a degree of definition with the man being seen as the earner of the income upon which the structure of family life depended. The role of the wife provides the chief dilemma in this suburb as she has the problem of devoting herself to her husband and children and still being socially conscious, of being an influential figure within the social life of Crestwood Heights both for her own satisfaction and for the status enhancement of her household. The children split their time between peer group activities, which are very important as Crestwood Heights is a strongly age-conscious community and the home and family corporate activities. The general view presented of the Crestwood Heights' family does not show greater family integration but rather a lack of integration produced by the rapidity of social change and the gulf between the members of the family which produces strains and conflicts. The families of Crestwood Heights are then nuclear units where the orientation of the family is towards both the child and the community; in the latter case the family operate as a unit in a status system. The actual influence of the suburb rather than other wider social changes is difficult to gauge accurately. Perhaps the central feature of this and other studies is that the suburb creates the opportunities and also necessitates some of the structural changes which occur. These may have occurred without the suburb, but in many cases the suburb does appear to have at least acted as a stimulant to change.

In studies of British suburbs attention has been focused upon the relation of the suburban family to its kin and the internal changes within the family which appear to have resulted from the move to the suburbs. Studies by Willmott and Young,[9] Bell[10] and the author suggest that in the suburbs between 27 per cent and 34 per cent of the families visit a parent each week. These figures represent a considerable reduction on the figures for the old-established working-class central city areas like

St Ebbes or Bethnal Green. Similar reductions in frequency of families visiting their parents are found in studies of working-class suburbs, e.g. Greenleigh and Becontree. So the reduction in frequency of contact appears to be uniform, and is related to the increased distance that the parents of the suburban families now live from their married children. The case of the middle-class family is rather more complex due to the lack of research evidence on middle-class family patterns in non-suburban areas. The middle class as a whole has always been more geographically mobile than the working class so presumably the linkages between the extended families of middle-class people have always been of a different order. Valuable insight into this particular group is given by a recent study by Bell. Bell studied two new private housing estates in Swansea and distinguished between middle-class families who were socially and geographically mobile and those whose whole life span had been within Swansea. In this latter case their parents and other kin were likely to be more important and to be seen more frequently. In the first case, these 'non-local' people attached more importance to the estate as a 'home' and had less frequent visits to their kin. However, the important finding which Bell makes much of is that their greater mobility does not necessarily affect the individual's commitment to his family or his reception of support from his or her parents. The families in the Swansea study in fact received considerable aid for house purchase, careers, and their children. This help was channelled through both parents hence this gave greater importance to the attachment of the families as complete units rather than as simply mother–daughter or father–son links which have been of most significance in studies of the working-class family.

These various patterns of family visiting have then an important connexion with the social class of the individual. This is shown by Willmott and Young and the author in their suburban studies. It was found for example in Woodford, that 26 per cent of the middle class compared with 42 per cent of the working class had parents living in the suburb. The middle class were found to keep in touch with their relatives who lived at some distance less by visit and more by means of telephone and letter, and so are able to maintain contacts without frequent visiting. The author's study found that the suburban dwellers with their parents living the greatest distance away were in the professional and higher administrative occupations and that as the social class of the resident declined so the number of parents living in the suburb or within a 25-mile radius increased appreciably. One further valuable point in this discussion can also be drawn from this study and that was the attempt to gauge the influence exerted upon visiting patterns by the suburb itself. Here there was found to be some evidence that the greater the distance the families were from their parents the greater was their identification with the suburb and the greater their involvement in the suburban life. It is perhaps also valuable to note that these various studies have shown little relative visiting apart from the parents of the suburban population and their brothers or sisters.

These changes in the relationship of the nuclear element to its extended kin has brought about certain changes within the family. The most important of these are that it has led to an increase in the amount of joint couple activity and the focus of the family moving to the children and their development. This increase in joint couple activity has been widely noted in studies of the suburbs. Willmott and Young, for example, quote the words of one of the Woodford wives where they write: 'In the old days, as one wife said, the husband was the husband and the wife was the wife and they each had their own way of going on. Her job was to look after him. The wife would not stand for it nowadays. Husbands help with the children now. They stay in the home, they have more interest in the home.'[11] Another area of activity where joint couple activity was noted was in visiting of parents. In Woodford Willmott and Young found that visiting of parents was nearly always a joint venture particularly where they lived more than twenty miles away. This joint activity in the suburbs is not just found within British suburbs but is also found in American studies, for example, in Levittown (USA). Gans found 40 per cent of his sample reported more couple visiting than in their previous residences and only 20 per cent reported less.

The suburban family which emerges from this discussion is one which has two adult members and one or more children.

This single type of family structure has had a number of consequences for suburban life some of which have been considered by the critics of the suburb as creating problems which need to be solved. The common type of family structure particularly as the families are to a large extent passing through the same stages of their life cycles together give to the suburb a high degree of homogeneity, which in its turn produces high rates of sociability. The prevalence of young children poses, however, other problems for the suburb such as noise and the providing of playing spaces. The restricted nature of family activities which results from the lack of extended family ties creates the most prevalent 'problems' of the suburbs for its critics: the problems of the loneliness, boredom and frustration of the 'captive suburban wife'. The picture which is presented here is of the commuting husband who is out of the house for five days a week at least from 8 a.m. to 7 p.m. in the London area, rather less elsewhere, leaving behind his wife and the small children. The society of the suburb, within which the young children grow up is, for the most part, female dominated and narrow and insular in its outlook. The topics of conversation at the 'coffee' or 'tea' sessions between the mothers in the suburb are either their respective husbands' careers or more commonly the latest methods of child rearing and their own family problems. In America the picture is painted of the middle-class mothers avidly reading the latest book on child rearing or the popular women's magazines in order to gain the initiative in the suburban status league. The frustrations and boredom are also related to the lack of opportunities for employment among the suburban women and the absence of nursery or other baby-sitting facilities to replace the role of the extended family to allow the wife a break from her house and the children to go out or to go shopping. This frustration is seen as most acute among the college- and university-educated middle-class wives who are found in the new suburbs as their expectations and demands upon life have risen through their education and also often through experience of employment prior to marriage and child rearing. The problem of adjustment to their new role of mother is exacerbated by the fact that the suburb is filled with other young mothers undergoing the same problems of adjustment probably just as unsuccessfully. The problem of loneliness has, hence, been one of the main consequences attributed to the decline in the extended family structure. Loneliness in the suburb, or indeed anywhere else, can be of a number of types and it is essential to keep these separate if any reasonable estimate of the extent in the suburbs is to be made. Three types of loneliness can be distinguished. Firstly, social which develops from a lack of friends; familial, which arises because of the separation of the children from their parents, and lastly chronic loneliness which is a form of personal alienation above and beyond social and familial causes. In his study of Levittown (USA) Gans found 28 per cent of his sample fell into one of these three categories of loneliness hardly making it a universal phenomenon. Of this 28 per cent, the majority (54 per cent) suffered from familial loneliness produced by leaving the cities and their families and moving to the suburb, 38 per cent suffered from social (i.e. lack of friends) and only 10 per cent from chronic loneliness.[12]

In the suburban studies considered earlier for Britain a decline in family contacts was noted in all cases where comparative data of the population before and after the move to the suburbs was available. Hence some degree of family loneliness would appear to be likely. In the case of the middle-class suburbs, e.g. Woodford, it is more difficult to assess as the whole pattern of middle-class contacts with kin is of a different order. The second question of social and chronic loneliness raises the question of the role of neighbours and friends in the suburbs. Have they replaced family contacts and so minimized family loneliness or have very few new social contacts been formed in the suburbs?

The role of residential location in the formation of neighbours and friends has been variously assessed. The suburb has for some writers provided a tremendous opportunity for the creation of new friendships based upon the suburb, and in fact has incorporated into it social values which dictate that this process of friendship formation by new residents is both desirable and expected. However, it is necessary to distinguish the kinds of relationships which arise on the basis of residential proximity which can be termed 'neighbour relationships' and those which are based upon homogeneity of backgrounds and interests which are essentially 'friendships', as they are likely to exist at a deeper level and persist over a longer period of time. The move to the suburb, the new house with its many initial settling-in problems, particularly in the case of the brand new estate, result in an initial phase during which relationships are developed. These are a result of the common 'problems' shared by the new residents, in disputes with the builder regarding the finishing of the estate or with the local council with regard to lighting or the siting of other facilities such as telephone kiosks or post boxes. These initial relationships are usually not sufficient in themselves to create intensive personal relationships between the families in the suburb unless they also coincide with other factors such as the families experiencing the same stage in the life cycle, hence share child rearing problems of a similar type, or where in fact there is a degree of homogeneity in the backgrounds and experiences of the suburban dwellers. The influence of the actual design of the suburb upon the initiation of relationships of a neighbour type is not easy to determine. Whyte in Park Forest[13] seems to believe strongly that the actual design of the 'courts' of Park Forest did lead to the greater development of social relations. Leo Kuper,[14] however, in his study of a Coventry suburb found no corroboration for the view that cul-de-sac design fostered neighbour relations. The extent to which neighbour relationships have developed has been related by some to the social class of the suburb where it is found that in the working-class suburbs relationships are still centred on relatives rather than neighbours hence rates of 'neighbouring' are much lower than in corresponding middle-class suburbs, hence the amount of loneliness could be higher. In the middle-class suburb, however, there is greater evidence of neighbour activity leading to the formation of friendships due to the homogeneity of backgrounds and experience which enable a continuing relationship to be established. This is the kind of suburb where the term 'quasi-primary' relationships has been used to describe these new patterns of friendships based upon physical proximity.

From a number of studies it is possible to see something of the extent of these relationships. In the study of Woodford by Willmott and Young they examine the pattern of friendships in some detail. They find that the friends of the sample are predominantly local and living in Woodford. There is a strong feeling that it is important for the individual to get out and make friends through being active in community activities. Within Woodford they found that the establishment of friendships on a neighbour basis was predominantly found in the middle class, the working elements of their sample did not have nearly so many friends, and even went so far as to express objections to allowing non-relations into their home. In the author's study of two middle-class suburbs it was found that 79 per cent considered it important to have good neighbour relations. However, the degree to which they knew them was not found to be very great, as although 80 per cent knew their neighbours well enough to have a chat, only one third would be willing to invite their neighbours into their houses. Also the number of neighbours known was quite small with only 11 per cent knowing more than six neighbours. There was found, however, to be some relationship between suburban identification and the importance attached to neighbours, indicating that this kind of relationship was associated by the individuals with a 'suburban way of life'. The study also found a similar relationship between neighbouring and social class to that found in previous studies with the higher social groups giving greater importance to neighbouring. One difference between the classes which may well have affected the figures for visiting is the tendency among the working class to have less formal visiting, the neighbours being much more likely to just drop in rather than visit in response to a specific invitation. The development out of neighbour relations of friendships is very important for the argument regarding the importance of the role of residential situation in friendship formation. It was found that 46 per cent of the sample had close friends living in the suburb and that these were visited weekly by over half. The basis of these friendships, however, was found to be quite varied with three principal sources of friends, work 33 per cent, neighbours 20 per cent and clubs and voluntary associations 22 per cent. This would indicate that residence was only one of the sources of friendships of the sample and not the most important one. The source of friends was also examined in relation to social class and here it was found that in all groups work was the most important source of friends (except the semi-skilled manual workers where neighbours occupied first place). This is not as would be expected as this is also the group with the highest number of relatives living within the suburb. The evidence from the study of social class and the source of friendships in the two suburbs studied thus shows that there is a relationship between these two, with the higher social class groups finding their friends from work and their involvement in various types of formal social activities, i.e. churches, social and sports clubs, and the manual workers finding their friends rather more in the neighbourhood. There is, consequently, a relationship as strong, if not stronger, between social class and the number, type and origin of friendships as there is between physical proximity and friendship formation.

There is, however, one other influence of the suburb upon friendship formation which has been cited by suburban studies. This is that the suburb engenders community-based activities which provide the source of friendships. For example, Whyte in Park Forest discusses the pressure exerted by the suburb upon the individual to join in the community social activities, to get out of themselves and join in with the crowd. It is seen in Park Forest as almost an offence against the community to withdraw or hold oneself aloof from social interaction with other members of Park Forest. Whyte, for example, quotes one of the residents as saying: 'Whenever we see someone who is shy and withdrawn we make a special effort with him.'[15] Whyte claims that the whole tenor of suburban life is becoming one which is explicitly communal, where the friendships are based upon physical proximity and involvement in community organization. A similar attitude to the one expressed by the residents of Park Forest is found in the Woodford study where Willmott and Young quote one of their sample as saying 'if you are not in the swim suburbia is hell'.[16]

The suburban critic points, as was noted earlier, to boredom, frustration and loneliness as a result of the move to the suburbs and the disruption of the family structure. Evidence to corroborate this view that these three changes collectively act to produce a rise in mental illness in the suburbs is not easily obtained. A study which has attempted this is by Benson[17] who studied family difficulties in a suburb of New Jersey (Morris County,

USA). The suburb chosen had a population of 25,000 and was twenty-five miles from New York. The occupants of the suburb were mainly professionals who commuted to New York. The average size of the households was 3·7. The total number of families included in the study was 433. The result shows only 10 per cent of the population to have problems of mental or emotional illness. Gans's study of Levittown also failed to provide any evidence of increased or widespread mental illness in the suburb. The belief that the suburbs of American cities were the scenes of mental illness appears to have had its origin in the novels written about suburbia in the 1950s which depicted the wives of suburbia as having mental and emotional problems for which they flocked to the psychiatrist for aid. The study of suburbs in Britain provides no real evidence on the question of whether the problems of suburban living which have been identified in respect to family structure and the wife's role have led to an increase in mental or emotional disorders. This perhaps indicates that this was not considered by the investigator as an issue important enough, i.e. prevalent enough, to merit separate investigation. There is evidence of role conflicts and of family strains but these are only partly, if at all, suburban in origin.

The role of the suburb in producing change in family structure is not a simple one. The increase of the domestic ethic noted in the last chapter has obvious and important consequences for the structure and activities of members of the family unit. The source of a substantial part of the changes in family structure observed in the suburbs is due to the influence of the geographical mobility experienced by the population. This movement cuts the family off from its kinship system which provided the basis for its previous set of social relationships and also a set of supporting services for the nuclear family. This, however, is only true of those who move from a stable working-class area to a new suburb. For many of today's suburban population the move is from suburb to suburb. They have already broken the ties of tradition and extended kinship, so the nostalgic looking back associated with the working-class population of places like Greenleigh clearly would not apply. Having cut themselves off, or reduced their association with members of their extended kin, the question then arises of how far quasi-primary relationships are created based upon living together in the suburb. Here there is considerable variation in the conclusions of the many studies with some like Willmott and Young considering that in Greenleigh the re-housed working class have not found many new friendships and little neighbouring exists. Instead the families are single isolated units where focus is still back in Bethnal Green rather than involvement in new activities in the new suburb. Park Forest of Whyte's study presents the opposite view where the middle-class population is seething with activity. Associated with these structural changes are those within the family to the roles of the husband and wife and to the increased importance given to the children. Coupled with these changes in structure and roles is, according to the critics of suburbs, a rise of certain social problems which point to dilemmas within the family in an industrial society. These are the uncertainties about the roles of parents in relation to their children which are exemplified in the study of Crestwood Heights; the loneliness, boredom and frustration of wives kept 'captive or housebound by the demands of their children'; the increased rates of mental illness and family breakdown produced by both the problems of parenthood in a situation shorn of its traditional kinship supports and the social pressures of living in a suburb and of being involved in its community influence. There is little evidence to support those who claim that these problems are caused by suburban living. The changes in the structure of the family where they occur are a product, primarily, of geographical mobility and this, because of the area where new housing has been provided, for most people means a move to a suburb. Hence the suburb as such does not exert any direct influence upon the initial weakening of kinship bonds. Second, the extent to which the residents of any suburb adopt patterns of non-family social relationships either through living in close proximity or through community-based activities depends for the most part upon their social class. The middle class in the suburbs studied do form neighbour relationships, which are in some cases translated into more far-reaching friendships where these coincide with other common factors such as occupation and stage in the family life cycle. Finally, the question of the extent of suburban social problems associated with isolation of the nuclear family unit. It is difficult to find any real support for the view that the suburbs are the scene of a great deal of social malaise and mental disturbance. Again evidence from the studies of both sides of the Atlantic rather suggest that where suburban populations have been carefully studied the incidence of these 'problems' is no greater than in the cities and may well, in fact, be less. Gans, for example, states most emphatically that it is more correct to speak of 'suburban happiness' than 'suburban malaise'.

The suburb appears to exert little if any independent effect upon the family patterns which prevail in the suburbs. It provides the conditions under which changes can occur perhaps more easily and rapidly than they would in either the city or the rural areas. However, the changes which promote the new situation which has been called 'the suburban way of life' centred around the family has causes which are external to the suburb and are to be found in the social class, geographic mobility and stage in the life cycle of the individual.

8 The Suburbs and Leisure Activities

The decline in the number of hours worked per week and the increased affluence of the population has given greater significance to leisure activities. This, coupled with the low proportion of the occupied population who find their satisfaction within their occupation, has led to an examination of leisure activities. The suburb has been seen by many writers to be the arena in which this increase in leisure and the solutions adopted can be most clearly seen, as here we have the most affluent, progressive and mobile sections of the population.

The discussion about leisure activities in the suburb has been clouded by the intervention into the discussion of the critics of suburbia, by the supporters of urban values which would be destroyed by the kind of leisure activities which they consider are characteristic of the suburb. These urban values defended by the critics are seldom made explicit, rather they are seen as the opposite of what the critics dislike in the suburbs. The writings on leisure in the suburbs present two contrasting ideas. On the one hand, the man in the suburbs is seen as increasingly privatized in his leisure, increasingly domesticated, centring his activity on the home or family.[1] This accounts for the rise in the popularity of do-it-yourself home improvements which occupy much of the new leisure time. This drive towards home improvement is seen as a status conditioned phenomenon, part of the 'keeping up with the Joneses', although the problem now appears to be which version of the 'Joneses' to emulate. This domestic-orientation of the suburban family is lamented by the critics as they see this as a sign that these families are little concerned with the wider community, with intellectual and cultural pursuits which would take them outside the four walls of their domesticity. In contrast to this view of the suburb is the one of the suburbs as 'frantically devoted to the rhythm of keeping busy', as 'hotbeds of social participation', and of 'communality'.[2] The suburb is seen by these writers to be suffering not from too little social participation and community activity but rather from too much, with too little individual privacy and not enough concentration upon the individual family unit and upon home-building. Whyte, one of the analysts of the suburb who supports this view, argues from his findings at Park Forest that the suburb's prime function for its inhabitants is to create for them a sense of belonging. The people moving into the suburb were all geographically and socially mobile individuals who had severed their ties with their family and community of origin, so they needed some kind of new community to provide them with support and compensation for their loss of familial ties. This sense of community is created for them by their extensive formal and informal social participation. The former is seen particularly in the role of the church in the suburbs which is highly successful and this is often ascribed to its stress upon sociability, upon the community centredness of its activities. The informal participation is shown by the yard social groups and parties of Park Forest or by the Kaffeklatsches of numerous suburban studies, the latter being social groups predominantly of women, meeting during the day while the men are away from the suburb at work. This kind of high participation leisure is also attacked by the critics for its apparent aimless quality, for what appears to them to be its frantic search for something to do which becomes a substitute for finding a satisfying way of life. Again the critics have seen this kind of suburban life leading to a lack of concern with intellectual and cultural pursuits which they ascribe to the city and see as integral urban values.

In order to clarify the discussion on the role of leisure, certain areas of non-work activity will be examined in more detail. The first of these is the extent of religious participation in the suburbs. There have been numerous writers in America who have been concerned with examining the growth of religious participation in the twentieth century, and various explanations have been advanced, including the influence of suburban living. The figures upon which much of the evidence for this rise in religious activity are based are somewhat contentious and some writers have claimed that what has happened is not a rise but merely a stable situation with the proportion of the population involved in religious institutions remaining fairly constant, although the absolute numbers have risen. Herberg,[3] however, has no doubts as to the existence of a rise in religious activity which he associates principally with two factors. The first is that third-generation Americans tend, as part of their integration into American society, to adopt the roles of Protestant, Catholic or Jew. The second factor, which is the one associated with the suburb, is the changing character of the American people. Drawing here on the work of Riesman, Herberg argues that 'other direction' has become prevalent among the new suburban middle class and that the return to religion becomes in part at least, a reflection of this 'other directedness'. Hence, joining the church in the suburbs has become one of the ways in which the individual is able to demonstrate to the rest of the community that he wishes to belong, to conform to the expected patterns of suburban behaviour and to adjust to his new community. The rise in religious participation can consequently be seen as, at least in part, a result of the rise in the need for conformity, so it is greatest in the suburb where this need is at its height. A survey of the involvement in the USA of the Protestant Church in both city and suburban areas has documented the progressive shifts since 1870 of the church and its congregation from the city to the suburb.[4] The growth of the church after 1870 was found to be very largely due to the attendant rise of the middle-class population. This has meant that, as the middle class left the city during the twentieth century, the church has moved out with them, resulting in a decline in churchgoing in the city and a corresponding increase in the suburbs. The contemporary suburban church is characterized in America by its identification with the middle class and by its adoption of an organizational style of activity. The debate about the church in the suburbs has often centred around the function which it now performs as a community organization. Much of the evidence to support this view is impressionistic. One study, however, which attempted to explore more closely why people joined the church in the suburbs found that for thirty-two out of the thirty-six joiners the reason was related to a consideration for someone else, usually their children.[5] It was because the family considered it was good that the child should attend Sunday School that they became involved themselves in order to support the child. This evidence for joining lends support to the view that the suburbs are strongly child-centred rather than the view that they are strongly religious. In this admittedly small sample there was little evidence that people turned to religion out of situations of distress. The figures available for church attendance and location in both Britain and the USA indicate that attendance is related to other variables than residence. Although the suburb as a whole has more church attendance than the city, attendance varies from suburb to suburb and in some groups the effect of the move to the suburb on their behaviour is greater than in others. This is clearly brought out in Berger's[6] study of a working-class suburb in America where he found 56 per cent never attended church and that for 49 per cent the move to the suburbs had no effect whatsoever on their religious participation. For those that it did affect, 27 per cent increased and 24 per cent decreased their frequency of attendance. For those that now attend more often it was found that they viewed the suburb as a more religious place than the city whereas those who attended less saw it as less religious. Similar evidence of only a relatively small number of suburbanites who reported a change in their frequency of church attendance is that presented by Gans[7] for his lower-middle-class suburb of Levittown, where he found only 33 per cent who reported an increase in church attendance. This change did not affect all the denominations equally as would have been expected in any general return to religion. The Jews in fact showed the greatest increase in attendance and the Catholics the least. However, Gans considers that purely social motives for church attendance were not very common. This would appear to challenge one current view of the church in the suburbs as a super social organization with not a great deal to do with religion. However, it is difficult to determine the extent to which people would be willing to admit explicitly social reasons for church attendance.

The whole discussion of religious participation is confused by the varying array of figures which are presented both by the religious organizations themselves and by social surveys and investigations of various types. One problem which always causes considerable difficulty is the difference between actual behaviour and a generally favourable disposition towards the church. The two suburbs in Bristol and Nottingham studied by the author showed 49 per cent who claimed to be members of a church, the majority of these claiming membership of the Church of England. The difficulty of finding any figures with which to make meaningful comparisons make it difficult to determine whether this is a high or low figure. However, a religious census was taken in 1965 of Bishop's Stortford,[8] which has had a rapidly rising population from 1951 as Londoners have moved into the town and increasingly turned it into a commuting area, so that this might be taken as a fair comparison. The study, based upon a 10 per cent random sample found that 95·5 per cent of the sampled population claimed some kind of religious affiliation, the largest category was that for the Church of England with 74 per cent. In this study, however, no examination is attempted of the frequency of attendance to discover how far this affiliation represents an active commitment and how far it is a fairly meaningless response. On the basis of these figures it is reasonable to conclude that the Bristol and Nottingham suburbs studied are less religious than Bishop's Stortford or that they are the average and it the exception. There is considerable, mostly impressionistic, evidence to suggest that the suburbs are the most flourishing areas in terms of church attendance and that the central city areas are suffering declining congregations but there is little in the way of accurate documentation based upon comparable definitions of membership and frequencies of attendance. The data in the Bristol and Nottingham suburbs were examined in relation to the extent of involvement, the social class of the individual and the degree of suburbanization. There was a steady decline in the number at each increase in the extent of activity examined. Of those who claimed that they were members, only 28 per cent attended church regularly, i.e. weekly, and of these just under half held some kind of office in the church (steward, churchwarden, etc.). Of the remainder a further 30 per cent claimed to attend church at infrequent intervals and the rest (42 per cent) attended rarely or never at all. This group's church activities tend to be associated with ceremonials like baptism, marriage and funerals. In terms of the whole sample the proportion of active members is consequently only 14 per cent which is considerably lower than the figure for those who claim allegiance in the whole sample (49 per cent) or the study quoted in Bishop's Stortford (95·5 per cent). There was a relationship found between claimed church membership and social class although this was not statistically significant, with the higher the social class, the higher the proportion of church members (see Table 4). The second relationship, that of suburban identification and church membership, again was not statistically significant (see Table 5). However, there was some indication of a trend, contrary to expectation, towards a higher proportion of members in the group with the least suburban identification. The data on extent of participation and social class tends to reinforce the findings of the higher social class groups being more active members. On the basis of the available data from the present study and other research work it is not possible to form any firm conclusions regarding the place of religious activities in the suburb. There appears to be some indication that the suburbs have more active church members than the cities and here the reason is very much tied up with the class nature of the suburb. The two studied here were predominantly middle-class hence the proportion of active members could well be much higher than if the population had been predominantly working-class. This conclusion is supported by the study of Woodford by Willmott and Young where they found that the middle class attended church more than the working class (34 per cent of the middle class had attended church within the last month compared to 17 per cent of the working class). They also found that the middle class provided the bulk of the office holders.

The second and related question is that of organizational participation in general. Here again the writings on the suburb have stressed the high rates of organizational membership, for example in Woodford clubs, and formal activities of this kind play a much larger part in the life of the individual than they did in Bethnal Green. These organizations like the religious denominations attracted the middle-class more than the working-class members of the suburb, (35 per cent of the middle class

Table 4

Social Class and Religious Behaviour

Registrar-General's Class Categories	Member	%	C. of E.	%	Methodist	%	Congregational	%	Baptist	%	R.C.	%	Other	%
I	32	57·1	24	75·0	1	3·1	2	6·2	2	6·2	—	—	3	9·3
II	29	50·0	22	75·8	6	20·7	—	—	1	3·4	—	—	1	3·4
III	45	47·9	33	73·3	3	6·7	3	6·7	—	—	2	4·4	3	6·7
IV	8	38·1	6	75·0	2	25·0	—	—	—	—	—	—	—	—
V	2	50·0	1	—	—	—	—	—	—	—	—	—	—	—
Total	116	49·8	86	74·2	12	10·4	5	4·3	3	2·6	2	1·7	7	6·6

TABLE 5

Suburban Identification and Religious Behaviour

Suburban identification	*Member*	%	*C. of E.*	%	*Methodist*	%	*Congregational*	%	*Baptist*	%	*R.C.*	%	*Other*	%
Least	35	60·34	26	74·3	6	17·1	—	—	1	2·9	—	—	2	5·7
Middle	35	46·6	24	68·6	2	5·7	1	2·9	2	5·7	—	—	6	17·1
Most	33	43·4	20	60·6	4	12·1	3	9·1	2	6·1	3	9·1	1	3·0
Total	101	44·2	70	67·9	12	11·8	4	3·9	5	4·8	3	2·9	9	8·7

had attended at least one such organization in the past month compared to 18 per cent of the working class).[9] The class differential within the suburb and between different types of suburb was also clearly seen in the work of Berger and Gans. Berger[10] found that 70 per cent of his working-class respondents belonged to no clubs or organizations and only 8 per cent belonged to more than one. Gans in his lower-middle-class sample found evidence of more organizational activity in 53 per cent and less in 7 per cent than the respondents had while living in the city, which gives some evidence of the move towards increased organizational activity within the suburban population. The interest of researchers has been directed not only to the total volume of formal participation but also to the kind of activities that have been important in the suburbs. One organization which is often singled out for attention in studies of suburban communities is the Parent–Teachers Association, an organization to which, we are assured by one investigator, everyone eligible in the suburb belongs. The reason for the importance of the Parent–Teachers Association in the life of the suburb is due to the high proportion of children of school age and the rising expectations of the parents for their children so that there is a strong demand for high quality education. The issue of the local educational system has been at the heart of many of the conflict problems within the suburban communities in the United States of America where the cost of education has risen rapidly, due to the demands of the families, and this has led to steep rises in local taxes which have angered original inhabitants of the areas and sections of the suburban population without children. The Parent–Teachers Association is, however, very probably an organization which is only widespread in the middle-class suburb. In Berger's study, for example, he found only 9 per cent of the men and 20 per cent of the women to be members of this organization. Willmott and Young also note the increased importance of the Parent–Teachers Association for the younger married couples with children but again their evidence seems to suggest that the membership is far from universal.

In the suburban communities studied at Bristol and Nottingham both the question of volume and type of activity was examined. Of the total sample 36 per cent were found to be members of some kind of organization. This overall figure was found to vary quite considerably when it was examined in relation to the social class of the individual. In the highest social class group 43 per cent of the sample belonged to organizations whereas in the semi-skilled working-class group this figure fell to 33 per cent (see Table 6). When the amount of involvement in these organizations was examined, this class differential was again very clear, with the higher social group having not only a higher total level of organizational membership but also a higher level of participation; and they were also members of more organizations and were more likely to be office-holders and committee members. This finding that both the volume and intensity of formal participation varies with class can be confirmed by most studies of organizational participation. For the suburban groups distinguished, however, there was little variation in the proportion of each group who were members of various organizations (see Table 7). When intensity of membership was examined there was some slight evidence of a negative relationship between high suburban identification and extensive

TABLE 6

Social Class and Membership of Clubs and Organizations

Registrar-General's Class Categories	*No activity*	%	*Low activity*	%	*Medium activity*	%	*High activity*	%	*Total*	%
I	32	58·2	1	1·8	10	18·2	12	21·8	55	100·0
II	39	67·2	1	1·7	11	19·0	7	12·1	58	100·0
III	62	65·9	3	3·2	19	20·2	10	10·6	94	100·0
IV	14	73·7	1	5·3	2	10·5	2	10·5	19	100·0
Total	147	65·0	6	2·6	42	18·6	31	13·7	226	100·0

χ^2 test is not significant.

TABLE 7

Suburban Identification and Membership of Clubs and Organizations

Suburban Identi- fication	*No activity*	%	*Low activity*	%	*Medium activity*	%	*High activity*	%	*Total*	%
Least	40	68·8	—	—	9	15·6	9	15·6	58	100·0
Middle	46	62·2	1	1·3	16	22·6	11	14·9	74	100·0
Most	52	68·4	3	3·9	15	19·8	6	7·9	76	100·0
Total	138	66·4	4	1·9	40	19·2	26	12·5	208	100·0

χ^2 test is not significant.

organizational participation. On the basis of this evidence there is little to support the view that there is a marked association between involvement in organizations and living in the suburb.

The question of what kinds of organizations the suburban dweller belongs to is also of some significance. Some thirty-four different clubs and associations were cited by the respondents. Not all of these, however, were based in the suburb. Some were located in the neighbouring cities, some were national associations which required little active participation on the part of the member. For the local-based activities the Women's Institute was most important for the women, with 10 per cent of the wives of the sample belonging. Other women's activities like Young Wives' groups attracted a further 5 per cent of the total. Political parties were not very strongly supported having a total membership of 6 per cent (Conservative 4·3 per cent, Labour 1·7 per cent). The Parent–Teachers Association was also not particularly well supported, with only 2 per cent of the sample being members. Overall the pattern of club and associational activities is a widely spread collection with no one activity standing out clearly as the activity of the suburbs as would perhaps have been expected from some, particularly American, writing. In the Bristol suburb, there was in existence a Community Association which attracted 10 per cent of the sample and was an attempt to provide for the whole community rather than merely particular sections as do the interest clubs and associations. In the light of this range of activities and the volume of members for each activity the figure of 49 per cent for church membership and even the figure of 15 per cent for active members suggests that the church is among the largest, if not the largest, single organizations in the suburbs studied.

A further aspect of this question of formal social participation in clubs and associations lies in the individual's involvement in sports and recreational activities and in public entertainments, theatres, cinemas, dances, etc. If the thesis of some of the critics of suburbia that the suburban dweller is becoming domesticated in his leisure is in fact correct, then increased suburban living should lead to a reduction in the support for mass entertainments and an increase in home-centred activities such as gardening and do-it-yourself. Some interesting data on trends in recreational activities are presented in a study carried out in the 1960s into the differences in the recreational activities of people living in Paris[11] and in the suburbs of the city. The study presents evidence as to the frequencies with which inhabitants of the city and the suburbs attend various types of public entertainment. They conclude that there are very considerable differences between the activities of city and suburban dwellers. The latter on the whole attend places of entertainment and recreation, cinemas, theatres, dances etc., much less frequently than do those living in the city. In many cases the differences are quite large, for cinema attendance they give a figure of 40 per cent of the population in the city and only 25 per cent in the suburbs and for the theatre 25 per cent in the city and only 15 per cent in the suburbs. This pattern of city–suburban attendance was also examined in relation to the social class group of the respondents and here it was found that there was a variation depending on the social class group with the higher the social class then the higher the frequency of attendance. However, in each of the class categories distinguished there was a city–suburban differential in the same direction as before. On the basis, therefore, of this evidence the suburban differential was clearly not subservient to that of social class. The distance of the suburb from the city centre is one of the main factors in reducing the amount of participation in city centre entertainments. The most popular form of organized recreation in the suburbs found in the French study were clubs and discos, cine-clubs, orchestras, parties and youth clubs. This was in contrast to the city where the most popular were given as dancing and the cinema.

Data on sports clubs and entertainments were also collected for the Bristol and Nottingham suburbs. In all, thirty different sports were represented in the replies. Again some of these were not ones associated with clubs but were highly individualistic, and some were not based in the suburbs. Of those that were, badminton 6 per cent, golf 7 per cent, tennis 5 per cent and cricket 5 per cent were the most popular. One leisure activity which comes under this general heading of recreations which has been strongly associated with the suburb is gardening. This activity is seen as part of the 'keeping up with the Joneses' status theme of suburban living. In Britain the popularity of gardening is fairly widespread. In a recent discussion of leisure activities it was estimated that over £100 million was spent annually on plants, tools, etc., and that this figure was increasing annually by 10 per cent.[12] How much of this increase has taken place in the suburbs is difficult to determine. From the survey evidence there were very few actually members of gardening clubs (3 per cent), however, there was a high response to the question of the importance attached to maintenance of the garden. The volume of participation in sports and other organized recreational activities was very much greater than that for other types of club examined earlier. The other aspect of recreational activity is that of public entertainment. The most popular form of this was the cinema (27 per cent). This was followed by theatre (23 per cent) and visiting the local pub (22 per cent). When this area of recreational activities was examined in relation to social class and suburban identification there was found to be a significant relationship in both cases, but the relationship with suburban identification was in this case the most significant (see Tables 8 and 9). With regard to social class it was found that the higher the social class, the greater the amount of activity in

TABLE 8

Social Class and Recreations

Registrar-General's Class Categories	*No activity*	*%*	*Low activity*	*%*	*Medium activity*	*%*	*High activity*	*%*	*Total*	*%*
I	10	18·5	7	13·0	36	66·7	1	1·8	54	100·0
II	16	27·6	7	12·2	34	58·5	1	1·7	58	100·0
III	30	32·9	11	11·8	48	51·6	4	4·3	93	100·0
IV	11	52·4	2	9·5	8	38·1	—	—	21	100·0
Total	67	29·6	27	12·0	127	55·7	6	2·7	227	100·0

χ^2 is significant as lies between 0·05 and 0·02 at the 95% level.

TABLE 9

Suburban Identification and Recreations

Suburban identi-fication	*No activity*	*%*	*Low activity*	*%*	*Medium activity*	*%*	*High activity*	*%*	*Total*	*%*
Least	9	15·8	7	12·3	38	66·6	3	5·2	57	100·0
Middle	21	28·4	13	17·5	38	51·3	2	2·7	74	100·0
Most	31	41·3	8	10·6	35	46·6	1	1·3	75	100·0
Total	61	29·6	28	13·6	111	53·9	6	2·9	206	100·0

χ^2 is significant as lies between 0·01 and 0·001 at the 99% level.

sport and public entertainment. This is similar to the French findings. In the case of the suburban group it was found that the greater the identification then the lower was the amount of activity. This finding together with the French study lends support to the view that the suburbs are the scenes of domestication rather than the outgoing life.

The activities of the suburban dweller are not only those which can be examined in terms of formal participation, particularly if the increased domestication of leisure activities hinted at above is in fact taking place. The evidence discussed so far does not present a picture of extensive formal social participation in suburban-based clubs and associations. The levels of activity are higher than are found for example, in working-class new areas but are hardly high enough to justify the claim that the suburb is a 'hotbed of social participation', unless there is a sizeable element of informal social participation taking place. One indication of the home-centredness of suburban living has been the growth, noted by many writers, of the cult of the handyman, who becomes increasingly involved in a whole range of home maintenance and improvement jobs, decorating, modernizing, building home extensions, car maintenance, etc. All these varied activities of the suburban family do provide an opportunity to enter into social relationships with neighbours who are also doing the same kinds of things and currently solving the same kinds of do-it-yourself problems. These activities also play an important role within the status system of the suburb with the 'keeping up with the Joneses' syndrome of rising aspirations and the desire to keep pace with and adopt the latest home improvements and household gadgetry. There is considerable documentation of this aspect of suburban life, particularly in studies of American suburbs. Whyte is, perhaps, the one who has done most to examine this aspect of suburban living, with his analysis of the social life of the people of Park Forest. In this study, he graphically describes the formation of social groups, based upon the courts, the clusters of houses built together, which are the representation of the new communal life which he sees as emerging. The social groups he sees not as novel groupings of the population so much as a projection of dormitory life and college sororities, through which the college-dominated suburban people have passed. In Park Forest there appeared to be four main types of resident. Firstly, the members of the groups who were the majority; secondly, those whose friendships tended to cut across the whole community, who consequently were not bounded by the court; thirdly, those who were intrinsically anti-social people who would be unable to get along with other people no matter where they lived and, finally, those who were seen as almost pathetically eager to be members of the group but who brought out all the bullying instincts in those about them, so in the end failed to achieve the one thing they really wanted – to be accepted into the group. These social groups, based upon the courts, were the whole basis for Park Forest's social and communal life, and groups developed their own distinctive character. Much of the informal group activity is primarily female, the male being absent from the community for the greater part of the day. The neighbourhood groups form, for daytime association, the morning coffee and afternoon tea circles where children's activities and husbands' careers are often the topics of conversation as well as the local gossip about the community. This kind of social community is highly visible both because of its group nature and also because of the architecture of modern houses which tends to have large open windows and open plan estates with few fences and little garden. Because of this visibility it is claimed that social isolation is difficult, if not impossible. Rather, social intimacy is promoted. The deviant from the dominant pattern of life is soon noticed and picked out. There is no longer the chance of being lost in the anonymity of the city. This then is the picture of the informal social life that is presented by studies such as Whyte's Park Forest, but how far is this true of all suburbs?

In other American studies of the suburb much emphasis is placed upon the round of parties as an important element of the informal social structure of the middle-class suburb. This kind of group activity is seen by Spectorsky to be the key features of his exurban communities in Westchester and Fairfield counties in New York State. These communities are the homes of America's mass communication experts, the advertising and television executives who live in these expensive, exclusive areas and try to forget about the intensive competition of their working lives. However, they cannot leave behind this competitive world, even in their leisure time. Spectorsky writes: 'All have something to do. All must have something to do. Each would feel he would sink to the level of a fifth-class power if the word got out that he was not invited out somewhere or inviting someone in.'[13] This view that at least certain suburbs are dominated by this round of intense social activity has given rise to the view that these suburbs are areas of dubious morality in which 'wife-swopping' becomes common, everything becomes subservient to 'the game', to the pursuit of fun and enjoyment, as a release from the pressures of modern organizational life. This kind of view is, however, more appropriately seen as part of the 'myth of suburbia', rather than the reality of the suburban way of life. This myth is neatly attacked by Gans[14] in a satirical essay about a man searching for this 'active social life' with its swinging parties and wife-swopping who moves first to one suburb and then another only to be told each time that this is what goes on in the next suburb. In the end, disillusioned, he returns to the city. Similarly, much of the supposed increase in anxiety, mental illness, status anxiety and general malaise are also more part of the myth than the reality of life in the suburbs and are portrayed principally by those who saw in the original idea of the suburb a return to the rural ideal and have since felt that this has been betrayed by the resulting mass suburb.

The informal participation in the suburbs has been examined by empirical studies which, on the whole, have found little evidence of large amounts of informal group activity. Berger,[15] for example, in his study found his evidence somewhat contradictory in that although 78 per cent said that they entertained friends at home, at least once a month, only 19 per cent reported being very friendly with their neighbours who constituted the largest group of their new friends. However, overall Berger concludes that for some of the women, at least daytime informal relationships have been developed with friends and neighbours; apart from this, visiting among neighbours is slight and where it does occur it is unlikely to have been arranged for a specific purpose. Studies of working-class housing estates in Britain have also found little evidence of large-scale informal social group activities, similar to that portrayed for Park Forest. In fact, rather than being 'hotbeds of social participation' many have been characterized as unfriendly places where people, on the whole, do not seem disposed towards establishing social relationships with neighbours, preferring to maintain existing family ties and participating in more anonymous leisure activities.

In the study of the Bristol and Nottingham suburbs some attempt was made to discover the extent of informal social participation. Of the whole sample, only 14 per cent said they belonged to informal social groups within their neighbourhood and most of those who belonged did participate quite frequently in their activities. The most common type was the female-based group, meeting during the day. When this activity was examined, in relation to social class and suburban identification it was found that there was a relationship between social class and informal participation but not suburban identification. The higher the class then the greater the amount of informal participation. There was double the amount in Registrar-General's category I (20 per cent) to that in category III (10 per cent) and only one case in category IV. This confirms that this kind of activity is primarily middle-class hence will be found only in middle-class suburbs.

The suburbs in America, but not in Britain, have been associated with one further important change which has become incorporated into the myth of suburbia in both countries. This is the influence of the suburb upon political party allegiances, resulting in a move towards conservatism by the newcomers. In the 1950s in both Britain and America there was a considerable volume of discussion regarding the changing nature of the political climate, with, in both countries, people arguing that there was a strong trend towards the more conservative party. This trend was given rather different explanations in the two countries. In America the explanation for many was found in the suburbs, 'the second great melting pot', whereas in Britain it was found in the increasing affluence of the working class.

The rise of Republicanism in America was associated with the period of the Eisenhower administration and the belief that in suburbia a quite extensive change was taking place which resulted in former Democrats of the city becoming Republicans in the suburbs. There were a number of reasons advanced for this change. The first was the kind of population redistribution that had taken place between the city and the suburb in which the higher income groups had been gradually vacating the city and moving into the suburbs and these groups were predominantly Republican. This has meant that the cities have become the preserve of Democratic administrators. The second change is the one put forward by Whyte that the suburb is the second melting pot where old identities are exchanged for new ones, old patterns of behaviour are dropped and new ones adopted and in this case the new identity and pattern adopted is that of Republicanism as this is seen as part of the suburban ideal. The third factor is that the movers to the suburbs represent the more socially mobile sections of the population. In one study, 51 per cent of the suburbanites were found to be upwardly mobile. These sections are willing to change their allegiance in order to facilitate acceptance by higher status social groups. Fourthly, the sub urbanite becomes, perhaps for the first time, an owner-occupier so becomes more concerned with issues of property rights, the security of his investment and tax levels and these lead him to support the more conservative party, which stands for lower taxes and greater stability. Lastly the great majority of the areas where new, particularly middle-class, suburbs have developed were originally strong Republican areas and so the local organization was better able to recruit support for the new population than the Democratic which had to start from virtually nothing.

There is considerable divergence of opinion as to the importance of suburban residence in changing party allegiances and also in the direction of this change. For example, in the study of party loyalties by Gruenstein and Wolfinger,[16] the conclusion is reached that all variation in voting between the suburb and the city could not be explained by other factors hence living in the new environment of the suburb did exert an influence upon voting behaviour. In another study by Manis and Stone[17] they found that only one out of every nine of their respondents changed party allegiance on moving to the suburb and all but three of these changes were from Democrat to Republican. However, they conclude: 'Compared with the importance of political climate, occupation and religion, suburban residence seems in itself politically irrelevant.'

Berger,[18] in his study, has shown that for working-class people moving into the suburb, the result is not an increase in Republican voting but a decrease. There was here also an increased interest in politics produced by their improved economic and social circumstances. Much of the difficulty of interpretation of the trends in political allegiance during the 1950s in America stems from the fact that Eisenhower was voted in as President on a personal rather than a party vote. This is illustrated by Manis and Stone[19] where they found 56 per cent of their sample were Republican party identifiers but 83 per cent were Eisenhower voters. Undoubtedly suburban residence has an influence in the complex of economic, social and residential changes which affect the socially mobile individual and lead to his adoption of a particular political party. The relationship, however, is not a simple one of suburban residence equals Republican voting. The relationship is, rather, suburban residence, social aspirations and economic situation equals the adoption of Republican voting.

In Britain there has been less emphasis placed upon the residence of the individual in seeking to explain the changes in party allegiance which were held to have occurred in the 1950s. These were the years of the dominance of successive Conservative governments with increased majorities. The explanations advanced have focused much more closely on the class structure and in particular on the thesis of embourgeoisement. This thesis suggested that it is the increasing affluence of the working class, or at least a section of it, which leads them to adopt the middle class as a reference group and consequently develop a middle-class style of life which includes Conservative party voting. This thesis was advanced by a number of writers but based on rather unsystematic evidence which was drawn from either selective studies of recently re-housed workers or workers in modern assembly-line industries or from opinion poll type attitude surveys.[20] The studies of the re-housed workers pointed to the influence of changed residential conditions (the people being moved to what is effectively a working-class suburb) in promoting behaviour changes in the direction of private or domestic activities and away from the extended family and wider community. This thesis was subjected, in the early 1960s, to a thorough-going investigation based on interviews with affluent workers drawn from three firms in Luton.[21] This study has not substantiated the thesis of embourgeoisement. The workers at Luton showed no evidence of large-scale changes in their political party allegiances and, in fact, showed stronger voting identification with the Labour party than is general in the working class as a whole. This lack of change is so even though many were now owner-occupiers, living in middle-class suburban areas of the town. If changes are occurring in political identifications then not just one factor is responsible.

The central concern of this chapter has been to examine the varying hypotheses concerning the extent of the suburban dweller's social participation. On the basis of the evidence it is very difficult to substantiate either the hypothesis that the suburb is an area where social participation and community organizational activity reaches an all-time high level, or that the suburb marks the beginning of a new kind of privatized or domestic type of leisure activity with the focus shifting increasingly to the home and family as the centre of these activities. Both of these hypotheses have some evidence to support them; neither has enough to justify the acceptance of one and the complete rejection of the other. The picture which emerges of the suburban man at leisure is of an individual who is mildly religious, who belongs to perhaps one other club or association in which he is more involved if he is middle-class than if he is working-class and whose wife is likely to be more involved than he in local social participation, both formal and informal. The suburban man's local contacts are, on the whole, spasmodic and of relatively short duration.

9 Myth or Reality?

The suburban way of life is a complex mixture of fact and fantasy which is extremely difficult at times to unravel, but it is essential for clear understanding that these two parts of the suburban way of life are clarified.

The growth of the myth of suburbia has been coincident with the physical growth of the suburb and has been most extensively analysed in America where it reached its height in the late 1950s. There are eight main elements of this myth in American society.[1] These are:

1. The suburb as a transient centre, the population undergoing a constant turnover with the average length of residence between four and five years. This is due to the composition of the suburb being predominantly young, upwardly mobile individuals (age span between 25–35 years).
2. The suburbs are uniformly middle-class areas with a well-educated population: both husbands and wives are usually college trained.
3. The population is homogeneous. This results from the one class nature of the population, the similarity of house design and the similarity of interests, with all of the families being at the same stage of the family cycle, at the same stage of their careers, all having just bought new houses and all busy home-making.
4. There is extensive social activity in both formal and informal participation, the latter taking the form of the Kaffeklatsches for the women during the day at which the conversation revolves around child-rearing and home improvements. In the evenings, the suburb is seen as the scene of parties and

dropping-in of couples for drinks etc., as a place with a considerable level of social activity.

5. Child-rearing is important and the latest authorities are taken as the guides rather than those of the extended family group. The fact that the husbands are mostly commuters means that suburban society is female-dominated and that child-rearing is very much the preserve of the woman.
6. There is a return to religion, the church performing social as well as strictly religious functions in the community.
7. Traditional Democratic voters become Republican.
8. The suburb is seen as the second 'melting pot' in American society where the upwardly mobile can learn the new norms of behaviour of the class to which they aspire in a community where the criterion of judgement is how the individual acts within the community rather than upon his social background.

In the 1960s this particular myth of suburbia was shown to be erroneous by the studies of Berger and Gans. These studies of a working-class and a lower-middle-class suburb have shown just how far divorced this myth was from the reality of many suburban areas. However, despite these efforts at myth-breaking, the myth has shown a great measure of resilience, continuing to dominate the thinking of many. The continued existence of the myth is due as much as anything to the fact that the critics of the suburb have become thoroughly caught up in their own creation. Donaldson writes: 'The curious thing is that much of the criticism which has been levelled against the suburb has been written by commentators whose thinking is far more powerfully influenced by this same myth than is that of the normally non-ideologically oriented suburban home owner.'[2] The preservation of the myth, however, despite the contrary evidence provided by sociological studies, shows the extent to which the myth forms part of contemporary American culture. It also supports the view that it is not based so much upon residential changes in American society as upon modifications and adaptations within the culture of the middle classes, of which Park Forest and Crestwood Heights are good examples.

In Britain the myth of suburbia has never received the same level of prominence nor the same volume of discussion but there does nonetheless exist a clearly held set of popular ideas regarding what constitutes the suburban way of life. This view, as in America, has often been somewhat derogatory with some viewing the suburb with disdain as the centre of the middle-brow, conformist, respectable uninspiring members of society who are quite content to potter around in their own rather limited world. This view is again somewhat divorced from the realities of suburban life. The suburb is a term which does for the majority conjure up a particular view of a residential neighbourhood with its rows of semi-detached houses cast in an identical, or nearly identical, mould and associated with this physical structure is a particular way of life. In both cases these tend to be stylized and often bear only a vague resemblance to the reality of life in the suburbs. This rather stylized view was illustrated by some of the respondents in the suburbs studied. In the Bristol suburb, for example, one respondent did not consider that he lived in a suburb as his house was not part of a new building development. Such a development, however, was taking place across the road from where he lived which he did term suburban, using the term in a somewhat derogatory way as if it in fact provided a well-understood and neat summary of undesirable features which were associated with new developments.

In the study of the two suburbs some attempt was made to investigate this particular aspect of the suburban controversy and discover what were the elements of the myth. This was attempted by presenting the respondent with thirteen elements which have formed part of the myth and finding out the degree to which the sample expressed agreement or disagreement with them. From their replies it was possible to build up a picture of what the majority considered to be the main elements of the suburban way of life. This way of life had seven elements. These were:

1. That is was a way of life which had a prevalence of and gave importance to do-it-yourself activities.
2. A central role to the family and child-rearing. These first two giving a picture of the central importance of familism as a major social value within the suburban image.
3. It was a middle-class way of life.

4. Great importance was attached to the possession of status symbols.
5. It was a life which was marked by a high degree of social activity.
6. It was strongly conformist in character.
7. Suburbs were politically conservative.

The picture which emerges appears to have a considerable degree of correspondence with what Riesman has described as the values of 'suburban peace and domesticity' with the consequent emphasis upon the work of suburbia rather than upon the work involved in the individual's occupation. The importance of home improvements is related to the familism of the suburban dweller but it is also related to another issue – that of status competition. It is claimed that people are motivated in their home improvements by a desire to have all the latest gadgetry to 'keep up with the Joneses'. However, in the survey, only a small proportion did, in fact, consider that suburban life was a 'keeping up with the Joneses' activity. An alternative explanation of the emphasis on home improvements is that this is a sphere in which the individual can, in fact, stress his individuality and seek to bring variety into his environment. The fact that the suburban dweller does not believe that the suburbs are depressing because they are identical in house design and estate layout suggests that it is an important aspect of the suburban life to produce variety through alterations to both interior and exterior design. One of the most striking things about new suburban estates is the speed at which variety is introduced. Again the conformity is perhaps more strongly in the mind of the critic than in the actual dweller in the suburb. The two popularly held notions or myths of suburbia depicted here for Britain and America show both similarities and differences. There is agreement, for example, on five of the elements, those of familism, the active social life, the homogeneity of the population, the middle-class nature of the population and political conservatism. There was, however, divergence on one key issue, associated strongly with the suburban way of life in America, that of the extent of transience. This was held to be a characteristic, if not the characteristic, feature of the American myth. However, only 24 per cent of the British sample cited it as an element.

The analysis of popularly held beliefs is only one aspect and one which often bears little resemblance to the actual activities of suburban dwellers. This gap between myth and reality is well demonstrated by Gans's essay on the man who frantically searches for the mythical social whirl of suburbia. In the suburbs studied at Bristol and Nottingham the important point which stands out is how little activity appears to be significantly related to the degree of suburban identification held by the individual. The most significant of these relationships concerned the lack of support for a non-instrumental view of work and an indication that this was replaced by involvement in the family and home-centred activities rather than widespread participation in social organizations. The picture which emerges does not provide evidence of massive and widespread social activity of either a formal or an informal nature nor does it show a tremendous amount of interest in such supposed suburban activities as religion, Parent–Teachers Associations or conservative political involvement.

From this examination of the actual activities of the suburban dweller and of the popularly held notions or myths it is possible to draw certain conclusions and inferences about the origin and perpetuation of the suburban way of life. It can firstly be seen that there is little real evidence that the simple fact of living in a suburb leads the individual to adopt a particular style of living. This can, of course, be broadened to say that any residential situation, be it urban, rural or suburban, does not of itself produce a way of life. The production of the way of life is dependent upon other factors but it may be that these are related to particular residential areas. The second thing which is clear is that the failure of many writers in both Britain and America to define clearly and to investigate the actual behaviour of people in the suburb has led to the growth and perpetuation of erroneous ideas. These ideas have been nurtured and developed for the most part because they correspond to the view of reality that some groups in society would like to exist, largely so they could then attack it as inadequate and in the case of America, as a betrayal of the 'American Dream'. Hence the whole edifice of the suburban myth is unsound and needs replacing by a carefully developed picture of what life is actually like in suburban areas. There is also the necessity to seek a more reasonable basis for the examination of the way of life in which people living in the suburbs share. Gans, in his study of Levittown, is concerned to show how the way of life of the people is a product of social class rather than the residential situation in the suburb. This is also the conclusion of Berger's study of Militipas where he found, within his working-class suburb, an adaptation of their previous working-class pattern of living rather than any move to adopt a suburban style as it is popularly believed to exist. The popular myth of suburban living is, consequently, seen by these writers as clearly associated with the middle class, hence it is correctly seen as not about suburban living but about middle-class life. The importance of this insight is considerable and when social class as a key variable was examined in relation to the evidence from the Bristol and Nottingham suburbs, it was found that for a majority of the questions relating to the three central themes examined, social class group either in objective occupational terms, or by self-assigned placement did show a much more significant relationship than did suburban identification. Hence this lends considerable support to the views of Gans and Berger that social class is a more significant variable in the determination of the style of life adopted by an individual than suburban residence. This relationship between social class and suburban imagery is further demonstrated by the significantly higher degree of suburban identification in the subjectively defined middle class. The popular image of the suburb in Britain, therefore, more correctly should be seen as a middle-class style of living than as a suburban style in that it is based upon occupational, educational and status criteria as much if not more than upon those of residence e.g. neighbourhood and house type. The adoption within the middle class of this particular style of life is not, however, universal. For example, there was found to be a negative relationship between the desirability of suburban life with the routine white-collar group showing the strongest support for the view that the suburban way of life is desirable. This lends some evidence to support, though by no means conclusively, the view that it is the middle-middle class to lower-middle class, those who have perhaps not been successful at getting to the top of their occupational ladders, who have moved to adopt the essentially family-centred ethic which has become, more or less, synonymous with the suburb; but, as discussed in an earlier chapter, the question of cause and effect here is difficult to determine as it could be that the adoption of familism leads to lack of success rather than vice versa. The essential role and hence value of the analysis of the suburb is that it is the place where the effects of these other changes can be clearly seen. The mistake of previous writers has been to confuse the causes of changes which lie outside the suburb with the effects of these changes which are increasingly manifest in the suburb and suburban way of life.

The Future Role of the Suburb

The suburb is rapidly becoming a world-wide phenomenon with the devolution of the major cities of the world as they grow increasingly congested. The continued importance of the suburb as a physical entity is assured for the foreseeable future, within the countries examined earlier, Britain, USA, France, Japan; although in both Britain and the USA there are those who argue that there is evidence of the beginning of a return to the city, but this has in neither country reached sizeable proportions. This is quite clear from the evidence of growth figures for the areas around the metropolises and the continuing population decline in the major cities of the world. What are the implications of this likely growth of the physical form of the suburb? The consequences for urban government and planning which are currently affecting many of the cities of America could well become the problems of Britain, if the cities decline to such an extent that they produce a marked imbalance in the population structure of the city. The suburban migration has been predominantly one of middle-class, higher income earners, coupled with the local authority re-housing of urban working class. This has resulted in the income of the city dwellers as a whole shrinking in times of rising expenses. This situation has led to considerable financial problems in American cities where the city's income is fast becoming inadequate to pay for the services the city has to provide. The other result of the selective character of migration is to leave pockets of particular ethnic or socio-economic groups in the city. In many English cities the migration to the suburb of the middle class from what were substantial and prosperous Victorian, middle-class residential areas has produced areas of large houses which have increasingly been taken over for a number of purposes, the most important of which is as multiple-occupancies for immigrant groups. The development of this kind of an area and its social implications are well documented in a study of Sparkbrook in Birmingham.[3] The creation of urban ghettos at their most extreme and local government financial difficulties are both in part related to the decentralization of the city and the corresponding growth of the suburbs. Neither of these has yet reached serious proportions in Britain but both could, before the end of the century, unless a constructive effort is made to counteract the existing trends.

Turning to the suburb itself, and its problems of planning and growth, Mumford's[4] attack upon the suburban way of life, raised in an earlier chapter, rested primarily on the grounds that what had begun as a valuable, thing when it was confined to only a small group, has been ruined by its own popularity. This popularity has destroyed the ideal and any virtues it may have originally possessed. However, in the two suburbs studied, of those who considered the areas to be suburbs, 56 per cent thought suburban life, i.e. presumably life as they lived it, to be desirable and only 22 per cent considered it undesirable. Hence, whatever the critics may think, the people who actually live in the suburbs do not appear to be too dissatisfied with the quality of their life. The suburbs do, in fact, offer an alternate arena to that of the individual's occupation and work organization in which he can find some kind of satisfying social role. This would appear to be all the more necessary where there is an increasing proportion of non-manual workers who are sharing the manual workers' instrumental view of work. For these people work is simply a source of funds and satisfaction is sought outside paid employment, not often in organizational activity of another type, but in informal social relationships based upon the family and in some cases the neighbourhood. The suburb, hence, could increasingly become the arena where people play their important social roles. If the analysis here is correct then the demands of the suburban dweller are not particularly complex as what he does not need are many extra-familial facilities as most of his time and energy will be devoted to the establishment and improvement of his house, homemaking and family life in general. Hence community facilities which require an organizational base, such as community centres, are not likely to prosper.

The confusion and contradictions which have bedevilled this area of urban sociology have, to a great extent, been due to a failure of diagnosis by the investigators, who have consistently failed to isolate the causes of the changes they have discussed from their effects. Once this is done, then the whole area of debate can immediately be clarified and progress can be made in the further investigation and elaboration of the varied styles of life which are present in each of the types of suburb distinguished. This means that just as there is not just one type of suburb, there is not just one type of suburban way of life.

Bibliography

Chapter 1. Introduction

1. P. L. Ford: (ed.) *Works of Thomas Jefferson*, Vol. IX, pp. 146–7. (New York, 1904.)
2. S. J. Low: 'The Rise of the Suburbs'. *The Contemporary Review*, Vol. IX. pp. 552–3. Dec. 1891.
3. Ruth Durant: *Watling A Survey of Social Life on a New Housing Estate*. (P. S. King, London, 1959.) This book provides a very good example of the cycle of development in community activities on new housing estates. See also R. N. Morris and J. Mogey: *The Sociology of Housing*, (Routledge & Kegan Paul, London, 1965).
4. S. D. Clark: *The Suburban Community*. (University of Toronto Press, Toronto, 1964.)
5. John Keats: *The Crack in the Picture Window*. (Houghton and Mifflin, Boston, 1956.)
6. T. Ktsanes and L. Reissman: 'Suburbia. New Homes for Old Values'. *Social Problems*, Vol. 7, 1959–60, p. 187.
7. A. F. Weber: *The Growth of Cities in the Nineteenth Century*, p. 475. (Cornell University Press, Ithaca, New York, 1963.)
8. L. Mumford: *The City in History*, p. 496. (Secker & Warburg, London, 1961.)
9. Scott Donaldson: *The Suburban Myth*. (Columbia University Press, New York, 1969.)
10. D. Riesman: *The Suburban Dislocation*. (Annals of the American Academy of Political and Social Science, p. 138, Nov. 1957.)
11. E. Howard: *Garden Cities of Tomorrow*. (1965 reprint with preface by Sir Frederic Osborn and introductory essay by Lewis Mumford). (Faber & Faber, London, 1965.)

12. ibid., p. 33.
13. Local Government Board: Report of the Committee on Building Construction in Connection with the Provision of Dwellings for the Working Classes, The Tudor Walters Report. (H.M.S.O., 1918.)
14. Royal Commission on the Distribution of Industrial Population, Barlow Report. Cmd. 6513. London, 1940.
15. For a comprehensive discussion of the background to and growth of the British New Towns see F. Schaffer, *The New Town Story*. (MacGibbon & Kee, London, 1970).

Chapter 2. Rural, Urban and Suburban

1. Registrar-General's Statistical Review 1960, Part I. p. ix.
2. G. B. Fawcett: 'The Distribution of Urban Population in Great Britain 1931'. (*Geographical Journal*, February 1932.)
3. E. Lupri: Rural–Urban Variable Reconsidered. (*Sociologia Ruralis*, Vol. VII, No. 1, 1967.)
4. P. H. Mann: *An Approach to Urban Sociology*. (Routledge & Kegan Paul, London, 1965.)
5. C. A. Moser and W. Scott: 'British Towns'. Centre for Urban Studies Report No. 2 (Oliver & Boyd., Edinburgh, 1961.)
6. ibid., p. 2.
7. H. Becker and H. E. Barnes: *Social Thought from Law to Science*. (Haven Press, Washington D.C., 1952.)
8. E. Durkheim: *The Division of Labour in Society*. (Free Press, Glencoe, 1960.)
9. H. Maine: *Ancient Law*. (Oxford University Press, World Classics, London, 1946.)
10. F. Tonnies: *Community and Association*. Translated and supplemented by C. P. Loomis. (Routledge & Kegan Paul, London, 1955.)
11. R. Redfield: *The Little Community and Peasant Society*. (University of Chicago Press, 1960.)
12. R. Frankenburg: *Communities in Britain*. (Penguin Books, Harmondsworth, 1965.)

13. L. Wirth: 'Urbanism as a Way of Life'. In A. J. Reiss (ed.) *On Cities and Social Life.* (University of Chicago Press, 1964.)
14. M. Young and P. Willmott: *Family and Kinship in East London.* (Penguin Books, Harmondsworth, 1962.)
15. H. J. Gans: *The Urban Villagers.* (Free Press, New York, 1962.)
16. See, for example, E. Rogers: *Social change in Rural Society, a Textbook in Rural Sociology.* (Appleton Century Crofts, New York, 1960.)
17. C. Arensberg and S. T. Kimball: *Family and Community in Ireland.* (Peter Smith, London, 1940.)
18. A. Rees: *Life in the Welsh Countryside.* (University of Wales Press, Cardiff, 1950.)
19. W. M. Williams: *The Sociology of an English Village: Gosforth.* (Routledge & Kegan Paul, London, 1956.)
20. W. M. Williams: *A West Country Village: Ashworthy.* (Routledge & Kegan Paul, London, 1963.)
21. J. Littlejohn: *Westrigg. The Sociology of a Cheviot Parish.* (Routledge & Kegan Paul, London, 1963.)
22. ibid., p. 111.
23. R. E. Pahl: 'Urbs in Rure'. *Geographical Papers*, No. 2. London School of Economics & Political Science. 1965.
24. D. C. Thorns: 'The Changing System of Rural Social Stratification'. *Sociologia Ruralis*, Vol. VIII, No. 2, 1968.
25. S. F. Fava: 'Suburbanism as a Way of Life'. *American Sociological Review*, Vol. 21, pp. 34–8, 1956.
26. G. A. Wissink: 'American Cities in Perspective. With special reference to the development of their fringe areas'. *Sociaal Geografische studies.* Hooglermar aan de Rijks-univirs. Zeit te Utrecht, Nr. 5, Assen Netherlands, Royal Van Gorcum.
27. W. Schärer: 'Die Suburbane Zone Von Zurich'. pp. 1–46. *Geographica Helvetica*, 1956.
28. S. F. Fava, op. cit., p. 37.
29. ibid., p. 37.
30. W. Martin: 'The Structuring of Social Relationships Engendered by Suburban Residence'. *American Sociological Review* XXI, 1956.

31. H. J. Dyos: *The Victorian Suburb. A Study of Camberwell.* (Liverpool University Press, 1967.)
32. R. A. Kurtz and J. B. Eicher: 'Fringe and Suburb Confusion of Concepts'. *Social Forces*, Vol. 37, p. 37, 1958, 1959.

Chapter 3. The Origins and Growth of the Suburb

1. Sir Leonard Woolley: *Excavations at Ur. A Record of Twelve Years' Work.* (Ernest Benn, London, 1954.)
2. Sir George Clarke: *The Wealth of England 1496–1760.* (Oxford University Press, London, 1946.)
   H. Heaton: *Economic History of Europe.* (Harper Row Ltd, London, 1963.)
3. H. J. Dyos: 'The Growth of a pre-Victorian Suburb. South London 1580–1836'. *Town Planning*, Vol. 25, No. 19, pp. 53–78, 1954.
4. Sir John Clapham: *A Concise Economic History of Britain*, p. 146. (Cambridge University Press, London, 1951.)
5. Sir George Clarke, op. cit., p. 113.
6. Asa Briggs: *Victorian Cities*, p. 80. (Odhams Books, London, 1964.)
7. J. R. Kellet: *The Impact of Railways on the Victorian City*, p. 376. (Routledge & Kegan Paul, London, 1969.)
8. See J. H. Johnson: 'The Suburban Expansion of Housing in Greater London, 1918–1939'. In J. T. Coppock & H. C. Prince (eds) *Greater London.* (Faber & Faber, London, 1964.)
9. Figures quoted in P. Hall. *World Cities.* (World University Library, London, 1966.)
10. H. Bellman: 'Building Societies, Some Economic Aspects'. *Economic Journal*, March 1933.
11. ibid., p. 25, table N.
12. H. J. Dyos: 'The Growth of a pre-Victorian Suburb', op. cit. p. 67.
13. J. R. Kellet: *The Impact of Railways on the Victorian City*, op. cit., p. 415.
14. J. T. Coppock: 'Radlett'. In Coppock and Prince (eds), op. cit.

15. A. R. Todd: Changes in the Metropolitan Countryside. Papers of a conference on planning for the changing countryside. (Town Planning Institute, 1967.)
16. Royal Commission on the Distribution of the Industrial Population, op. cit.
17. P. Abercrombie and J. H. Forshaw: *County of London Plan.* (Macmillan, London, 1943.)
18. D. A. Reeder: 'A Theatre of Suburbs. Some Patterns of Development in West London. 1801–1911'. In H. J. Dyos (ed.) *Studies in Urban History.* (Edward Arnold Ltd, London, 1968.)
19. ibid., p. 259.
20. H. J. Dyos: *The Victorian Suburb. A Study of Camberwell,* op. cit.
21. Ruth Glass: Introduction in R. Glass (ed.) *London Aspects of Change.* Centre for Urban Studies. Report No. 3. (MacGibbon & Kee, London, 1964.)
22. J. Aiken: *A Description of the Country from thirty to forty-miles round Manchester.* (Stockdale, London, 1795. Reprinted Kelley, 1968.)
23. Asa Briggs: *Victorian Cities,* op. cit., p. 147.
24. C. A. Moser and W. Scott: 'British Towns', op. cit.
25. T. W. Freeman: The Conurbations of Great Britain, (Manchester, 1969.) The Manchester Conurbation. British Association for the Advancement of Science. *Scientific Survey.* Manchester, 1962.
26. C. Moindrot: 'The Movement of Population in the Birmingham Region'. In C. J. Jansen (ed.) *Readings in the Sociology of Migration.* (Pergamon Press, Oxford, 1970.)
27. L. Mumford: *The City in History,* op. cit., p. 486.

Chapter 4. The Growth and Development of the Suburbs: United States, France and Japan

1. Figures drawn from P. Hall: *World Cities,* op. cit.
2. A. F. Weber: *The Growth of Cities in the Nineteenth Century,* op. cit.

3. D. W. Kirk: Some Reflections on American Democracy in the Nineteen Sixties. *Population Index. XXVI*, October 1960, p. 306.
4. S. B. Warner: *Street Car Suburb.* (Harvard University Press, 1962.)
5. H. P. Douglass: *The Suburban Trend.* (The Century Co., New York, 1925.)
6. ibid., p. 68, Table 15.
7. Figures drawn from L. F. Schnore: 'Municipal Annexations and the Growth of Metropolitan Suburb. 1950–60.' *American Journal of Sociology*, Vol. 67, pp. 406–17, 1961–2.
A. H. Hawley: *The Changing Shape of Metropolitan America.* (Free Press, Glencoe, Illinois, 1956.)
D. J. Bogue: Population Growth in the Standard Metropolitan Areas, 1900–1950. Washington D.C. Housing and Home Finance Agency, 1953.
8. Samuel Swift: 'Llewellyn Park, Orange, New Jersey'. In *House and Garden*, Vol. III, No. 6. pp. 327–35.
9. The designers of Central Park, New York.
10. J. Keats: *The Crack in the Picture Window*, op. cit.
11. Figures quoted in G. A. Wissink: *American Cities in Perspective*, op. cit., p. 233.
12. United States Government Commission.
13. A. F. Parrott: 'Flight to the Suburb Slackens'. Proceedings of the social statistics section of the American Statistical Association. 1960. pp. 152–8.
14. Figures from A. F. Weber, op. cit., p. 67.
15. P. George: Études sur la banlieue de Paris. Ch. III. *Études Demographique.* (Librairie Armand Colin, Paris, 1950.)
16. C. Cornau, M. Imbert, B. Lamy, P. Rendu and J. Retel: *L'attraction de Paris sur sa banlieue.* Ch. I. (Édition Ouvrièries, Paris, 1965.)
17. P. George, op. cit., p. 20.
18. Figures drawn from:

P. Hall, op. cit. Chapter on Tokyo.
I. B. Taeuber: 'Urbanisation, Population Change in the Development of Modern Japan'. *Economic Development and Cultural Change*, Vol. 9, No. 1, Part II, 1960.

A. W. Burks: 'The City Political Change and Modernisation in Japan'. *International Journal of Comparative Sociology*, Vol. 7, No. 1, March 1966.
D. H. Kornhauser: 'Urbanisation and Population Pressure in Japan'. *Pacific Affairs*, pp. 275–85, 1958.

19. Quoted in A. W. Burks, op. cit., pp. 41–2.
20. Sen Matsuda: 'The Salaried Man in Japan'. *Hemisphere II.* pp. 9–15, July 1967.
21. P. Hall, op. cit., p. 231.
22. R. P. Dore: *City Life in Japan.* (Routledge & Kegan Paul, London, 1958.)

Chapter 5. Types of Suburb

1. W. M. Dobriner: *Class in Suburbia.* Ch. 5. (Prentice Hall, New Jersey, 1963.)
2. A. C. Spectorsky: *The Exurbanites.* (J. P. Lippincott & Co., Philadelphia, 1955).
3. H. J. Gans: *The Levittowners.* Ch. 3. (Allen Lane The Penguin Press, London, 1967.)
4. W. H. Whyte: *The Organization Man*, Part 7. (Jonathan Cape, London, 1957 and Penguin Books, Harmondsworth, 1961.)
5. J. R. Seeley, R. A. Sim, and E. W. Loosley: *Crestwood Heights.* (Basic Books, New York, 1956.)
6. B. Berger: *Working-class Suburb.* Ch. 1, pp. 11–14. (University of California Press, Berkeley, and Los Angeles, 1960.)
7. P. Willmott and M. Young: *Family and Class in a London Suburb.* (New English Library. Mentor Edition, London, 1967.)
8. H. P. Douglass: *The Suburban Trend*, op. cit. Ch. 3.
9. C. D. Harris: 'Suburbs'. *American Journal of Sociology*, Vol. XLIX, 1943.
10. S. D. Clark: *The Suburban Community*, op. cit.
11. P. Willmott: *The Evolution of the Community.* Ch. I. (Routledge & Kegan Paul, London, 1963.)

12. W. Ashworth: Types of Social and Economic Development in Suburban Essex. In R. Glass (ed.) *London Aspects of Change*, op. cit.
13. C. Moser and W. Scott: 'British Towns', op. cit.

List of studies referred to in Table 3

14. Whyte, W. H.: *The Organization Man.*
15. Ziell, T.: 'Social Change in Levittown'. In Dobriner, W. M. (ed.), *Class in Suburbia.*
16. Sim, *et al.*: *Crestwood Heights.*
17. Willmott, P. and Young, M.: *Family and Class in a London Suburb.*
18. Berger, B.: *Working-class Suburb.*
19. Young, M. and Willmott, P.: *Family and Kinship in East London* (Part II).
20. Elias, N. and Scotson, J. T.: *The Established and Outsider.*
21. Willmott, P.: *The Evolution of a Community.*
22. Dobriner, W. M.: 'The natural history of a Reluctant Suburb' In Class in Suburbia, ed., W. M. Dobriner.
23. Pahl, R. E.: 'Urbs in Rure', op. cit.
24. Thorns, D. C.: 'The Changing System of Rural Social Stratification', *Sociologia Ruralis*, 1968.
25. Crichton, R.: *Commuter's Village* (David and Charles, 1964.)
26. Spectorsky, A. C.: *The Exurbanites*, op. cit.
27. Mitchell, G. D. and Lupton, T.: *Neighbourhood and Community*. (Liverpool University Press, Liverpool, 1954.)
28. Ashworth, W.: *The Genesis of Modern Town Planning.* (Routledge & Kegan Paul, 1954.)
29. Dyos, H.: *The Victorian Suburb. A Study of Camberwell.* op. cit.
30. Clark, S. D.: *Suburban Society* (in which examples of most of the types distinguished), op. cit.

31. L. Mumford: *The City in History*, op. cit., p. 215.
32. W. H. Whyte, *The Evolution of the Community,* op. cit., p. 258.
33. P. Willmott, *The Organization Man,* op. cit., p. 4.
34. ibid., p. 89.

35. J. Mogey: *Family and Neighbourhood.* (Oxford University Press, London, 1956.)
H. Jennings: *Societies in the Making.* (Routledge & Kegan Paul, London, 1962).
M. Young and P. Willmott: *Family and Kinship in East London*, op. cit.
36. W. M. Dobriner, op. cit. Ch. 5, The Natural History of a Reluctant Suburb. p. 133.
37. R. E. Pahl: 'Urbs in Rure', op. cit.
38. ibid., p. 45.
39. D. C. Thorns: 'The Changing System of Rural Social Stratification', op. cit.
40. G. D. Mitchell and T. Lupton: *Neighbourhood and Community. See* the Liverpool Estate, op. cit.
41. See for example, P. George: *Études sur la banlieue de Paris*, op. cit. and also C. Chabot. *Faubourgs, banlieuex et zones d'influence, urbanisme et habitation*, 1954.
42. R. E. Pahl, op. cit., p. 47.
43. R. L. Thomas: London's New Towns. A study of self contained and balanced communities. P.E.P. Broadsheet 510, Vol. XXXV, London, 1969.
44. B. J. Heraud: Social Class and the New Towns. *Urban Studies*, Vol. 5, No. 1, 1968.

Chapter 6. The Suburbs and Work Ethics

1. Max Weber: *The Protestant Ethic and the Spirit of Capitalism.* (Translated Parsons, Allen & Unwin, London, 1930).
2. W. H. Whyte: *The Organization Man*, op. cit. pp. 11–12.
3. R. Dubin: 'Industrial Workers' Worlds. A Study of Central Life Interests of Industrial Workers'. *Social Problems*, Vol. 5, pp. 131–42, 1956.
4. R. Weiss and R. Kahn: 'Definition of Work and Occupation'. *Social Problems*, Vol. 8, No. 2, pp. 142–51, 1960.
5. E. A. Friedman and R. J. Havighurst: 'Work and Retirement'. In S. Nosow and W. H. Form (eds), *Man, Work and Society. A Reader in the Sociology of Occupation.* (Basic Books Inc., New York, 1962.)

6. Ely Chinoy: *Automobile Workers and the American Dream.* (Doubleday & Co. Inc. Garden City, New York, 1955.)
7. B. Berger: *Working-class Suburb*, op. cit.
8. J. H. Goldthorpe, D. Lockwood, F. Bechofer and J. Platt: *The Affluent Worker. Industrial Attitudes and Behaviour.* (Cambridge University Press, 1968.)
9. F. Zweig: *The British Worker.* (Penguin Books, Harmondsworth, 1952.); *The Worker in the Affluent Society.* (Heinemann, London, 1961.)
10. M. Young and P. Willmott: *Family and Kinship in East London*, op. cit.
11. R. Dubin, op. cit., p. 135.
12. F. Zweig: *The British Worker*, op. cit. p. 97.
13. P. Willmott: *The Evolution of the Community*, op. cit.
14. N. C. Morse and R. S. Weiss: 'The Function and Meaning of Work and the Job'. *American Sociological Review*, Vol. 20, April 1955, pp. 191–8.
15. J. R. Seeley, R. A. Sim and E. W. Loosley: *Crestwood Heights*, op. cit., p. 130.
16. ibid., p. 185.
17. L. H. Orzack: 'Work as a Central Life Interest of Professionals'. *Social Problems*, Vol. 7, No. 2, 1959.
18. S. Cotgrove: 'The Relations Between Work and Non Work Among Technicians'. *Sociological Review*, Vol. 13, pp. 121–9, 1965.
19. K. Prandy: *Professional Employees.* (Faber & Faber, London, 1965.)
20. W. H. Whyte, op. cit.
21. D. Riesman: *The Suburban Dislocation*, op. cit.

Chapter 7. The Suburb and the Family

1. W. Bell: 'Familism and Suburbanisation'. *Rural Sociology*, Vol. 21, pp. 276–83, 1956.
2. B. E. Munson: 'Attitudes towards Urban and Suburban Residence in Indianapolis'. *Social Forces*, Vol. 35, pp. 76–80, 1956.
3. H. J. Gans: *The Levittowners*, op. cit.

4. M. Young and P. Willmott: *Family and Kinship in East London*, op. cit.
5. W. E. Mowrer: 'The Family in Suburbia', in W. H. Dobriner (ed.) *The Suburban Community*. (G. P. Putnam & Sons, New York, 1958.)
6. ibid., p. 152.
7. J. R. Seeley, R. A. Sim and E. A. Loosley: *Crestwood Heights*, op. cit.
8. ibid., p. 46.
9. M. Young and P. Willmott: *Family and Class in a London Suburb*, op. cit.
10. C. Bell: *Middle Class Families*. (Routledge & Kegan Paul, London, 1968.)
11. P. Willmott and M. Young, op. cit., p. 29.
12. H. J. Gans: *The Levittowners*, op. cit. pp. 230–31.
13. W. H. Whyte: 'The Outgoing Life. The Transients, Part III'. *Fortune*, July 1953.
14. Leo Kuper (ed.): *Living in Towns*. (Cresset Press, London, 1953.)
15. W. H. Whyte: 'The Outgoing Life', op. cit., p. 89.
16. P. Willmott and M. Young, op. cit., p. 95.
17. P. H. Benson, A. Brown and L. M. Sheeney: 'A Survey of Family Difficulties in a Metropolitan Suburb'. *Marriage and Family Living*, pp. 249–53, August 1956.

Chapter 8. The Suburb and Leisure Activities

1. See for example the writings of D. Riesman.
2. See for example the writings of W. H. Whyte.
3. W. Herberg: 'The Contemporary Upswing to Religion', in N. Birnbaum and G. Lenser (eds). *Sociology of Religion*. (Prentice Hall, Englewood Cliffs, New Jersey, 1969.)
4. G. Winter: *The Suburban Captivity of the Churches*. (Doubleday Inc., Garden City, New York.)
5. D. Nash and P. Berger: 'The Child, the Family and the Religious Revival in Suburbia'. *Journal of the Scientific Study of Religion*, Vol. 2, pp. 85–93, 1962.
6. B. Berger: *Working-class Suburb*, op. cit., pp. 44–8.

7. H. J. Gans: *The Levittowners*, op. cit., pp. 256–7, Table 7.
8. A. Spencer: Religious Census of Bishop's Stortford, pp. 135–45. In D. Martin (ed.) *A Sociological Yearbook of Religion in Britain.* (S.C.M. Press, London, 1968.)
9. P. Willmott and M. Young, op. cit., p. 82, table XIII.
10. B. Berger, op. cit., pp. 54–80.
11. C. Cornau, *et al.*, *L'attraction de Paris sur sa banlieue*, op. cit., pp. 131–4.
12. 'All Work and No Play', *Woman*, Vol. 66, No. 1724, June 1970, p. 31.
13. A. C. Spectorsky: *The Exurbanites*, op. cit., p. 191.
14. H. J. Gans: *People and Plans. Essays on Urban Problems and Solutions.* (Basic Books, New York, 1968.)
15. B. Berger: op. cit., pp. 64–73.
16. F. I. Gruenstein and R. E. Wolfinger: 'The Suburb and Shifting Party Loyalties'. *Public Opinion Quarterly*, Vol. 22, No. 4, 1958–9, p. 475.
17. J. G. Manis and L. C. Stone: 'Suburban Residence and Political Behaviour'. *Public Opinion Quarterly*, Vol. 22, No. 4, 1958–9, pp. 483–9.
18. B. Berger: op. cit., Ch. III, Republicans or Democrats? pp. 28–39.
19. J. G. Manis and L. C. Stone, op. cit., p. 484.
20. J. H. Goldthorpe and D. Lockwood: 'Affluence and the British Class Structure'. *Sociological Review* n.s. Vol. 11, 1963.
21. J. H. Goldthorpe, *et al.*: 'The Affluent Worker'. *Sociology* Vol. 1, No. 1, pp. 11–31, 1967.

Chapter 9. Myth or Reality?

1. See W. M. Dobriner: *Class in Suburbia*, op. cit., Ch. 1, Scott Donaldson *The Suburban Myth*, op. cit. and B. Berger, *Working-class Suburb*, op. cit., Ch. 1.
2. Scott Donaldson, op. cit., p. 17.
3. J. Rex and R. Moore: *Race and Community.* (Oxford University Press, London, 1967.)
4. L. Mumford: *The City in History*, op. cit., Ch. 16.

Index